THE 1923 GRECO-TURKISH POPULATION EXCHANGE: SUCCESSFUL PREVENTION OF GENOCIDE AND MASS ATROCITIES

ABSTRACT

THE 1923 GRECO-TURKISH POPULATION EXCHANGE: SUCCESSFUL
PREVENTION OF GENOCIDE AND MASS ATROCITIES, by Major Jason B.
Faulkenberry, 110 pages.

This thesis is a case study of the 1923 Greco-Turkish population exchange and asserts the
compulsory expulsion effectively prevented genocide of Orthodox Christians living in
Asia Minor. To support this argument historical evidence leading up to the exchange is
presented and examined for specific genocide indicators. Contemporary terms and
viewpoints of genocide and mass atrocities are used to assess the historical facts and
support the hypothesis. The study further addresses the long-term results of the exchange.
This study is focused only on the events that support the thesis and does not examine
wider sociological and historical context. It is by no means a comprehensive history of
Greece and Turkey following World War I. Furthermore, it does not attempt to examine
the logistics of the exchange but provides a broad understanding of the process. The
thesis concludes the population exchange and the associated treaty ended the Greco-
Turkish conflict and ensured a lasting peace in a relative volatile region. Although it
violated individual rights and had deleterious effects on Greece's economy, it was
necessary to prevent future mass atrocities and potential genocide

ACKNOWLEDGMENTS

First, I would like to thank my wife Melody, who spent many weekends entertaining my son so I could research and write. I also want to acknowledge my committee members Dr. Charles Heller, Mr. Dale Spurlin and Mr. Michael Weaver. Their mentorship, motivation, assistance and patience guided me each step of the way and provided great insight. This thesis would not have been possible without their input. Their involvement made this experience memorable and most importantly, educational.

TABLE OF CONTENTS

ACRONYMS

U.S.   United States

WWI   World War I

ILLUSTRATIONS

CHAPTER 1

INTRODUCTION

There is no greater sorrow on earth than the loss of one's native land
— Euripides

Kayaköy is the name of a ghost village located on a mountainside of coastal Turkey. The village consists of several hundred empty houses, churches and other buildings scattered about an idyllic landscape. The sun kissed Mediterranean climate only adds to the uneasy feeling the vacancy brings. Dilapidated structures and overgrown vegetation cannot sufficiently hide the greatness of the civilization that once flourished in these lands. The brick and mortar buildings built to withstand any natural calamity have weathered time successfully. In the end, the structures endured several natural disasters but succumbed to human tragedy. All of the village's inhabitants were expelled in 1923 as part of a controversial peace treaty and population exchange between Greece and Turkey.[1]

Following World War I (WWI) a short-lived Greco-Turkish war erupted, resulting in a series of atrocities committed by both nations. Once hostilities ended, the two governments agreed to exchange the Greek and Turkish minorities residing within their respective countries. The population exchange was mandated by the "Convention Concerning the Exchange of Greek and Turkish Populations" signed in Lausanne, Switzerland on 30 January 1923. The forced expulsion of the minorities was solely based on religious identity and involved approximately 1.2 million Greek Orthodox and

---

[1]"The idyllic town that time forgot," *The Independent*, 11 June 2005.

1

300,000 Muslim citizens.[2] At the time, the mass expulsion also known as ethnic engineering was lauded as the only viable solution for minorities that could not coexist. Unfortunately, the exchange had unprecedented and broad results for the individuals and the nations involved.[3]

The 1923 population exchange was unique in many ways. The destinies of Aristotle Onassis, Ernest Hemingway and Medal of Honor recipient Private First Class George Dilboy are interwoven with the million and a half other emigrants in this unique historical event. The convention for the exchange and the wider Lausanne Treaty ended the conflict between Greece and Turkey but further prevented potential genocide of Greek Orthodox Christians living in Asia Minor. Unbeknownst to the delegates of the time, several indicators of genocide existed hinting to the ensuing crimes against humanity.[4] In that respect, this population exchange, despite the negative aspects, had a positive outcome as it prevented genocide. The examination of this event should also prompt key leaders to reconsider forced population transfers.

Up until the mid-twentieth century, forced population migration or deracination, was considered a viable and often necessary solution to ethnic conflicts. Due to poor execution and the belligerent manner of past population transfers, the practice is presently frowned upon and discontinued. However, current ethnic/religious divisions prevalent in

---

[2]Alexis Alexandris, "Religion or Ethinicity: Identity of the Minorities," in *Crossing the Aegean: An Appraisal of the 1923 Compulsory Population Exchange Between Greece and Turkey*, ed. Renee Hirschon (New York: Oxford, 2008), 117.

[3]Lausanne Peace Treaty VI (Convention concerning the Exchange of Greek and Turkish Populations and Protocol, signed at Lausanne 30 January 1923).

[4]Silas Bent, "Uprooting of Greeks in Turkey A Modern Exodus of Outcasts," *The New York Times*, 21 January 1923.

many countries around the world provide fertile ground for conflict with few apparent solutions. The Greco-Turkish population exchange demonstrated first that such a herculean endeavor could be accomplished. It further ensured peace in a rather volatile region. Lastly it indicated that although it is preferred to have minorities coexist harmoniously, sometimes the only way to have peace is to separate the belligerent groups.[5]

Research Questions and Methodology

The aim of this thesis is to study one primary and two secondary research questions. The primary question is: Did the 1923 Greco-Turkish population exchange prevent genocide? This led to two secondary research questions. Why was the population exchange considered? What were the lasting implications of the exchange?

The primary methodology used for answering these questions was the study of documents outlining the events leading to and including the population exchange. Additionally this study used several books authored by sociologist, historians and politicians who have studied the events of 1923. Many of the books include interviews or firsthand accounts of the events described. Other works are journals of individuals witnessing the events. This thesis illustrates the events leading up to the population exchange but can also provide great insight on the forging of the modern nations of Greece and Turkey. Finally, this thesis elaborates on the past and current Greco-Turkish relationship and ongoing points of contention.

---

[5]Renee Hirschon, *Crossing the Aegean: An Appraisal of the 1923 Compulsory Population Exchange Between Greece and Turkey* (New York: Oxford, 2008), 9-12.

Thesis

History is filled with forced population expulsions most of which were under hostile circumstances. In the past, population expulsions were used to rid territories of threatening groups that might disrupt the consolidation of political power. In order to enforce social homogeneity, populations were selected for forced migrations based on ethnicity or religion. Due to the contentious environment that such exchanges took place, the execution and results were often negative if not detrimental to the affected populations and the nations involved. As a result, compulsory population migrations, which were commonplace in the past, became unpopular following World War II. Critics often mention the controversial legal issues, violations of individual rights, and the failed historical examples as arguments against such measures. These critics, however, place more emphasis on ethical considerations rather than pragmatic results.[6]

The Lausanne Treaty and the Convention to exchange populations ended the Greco-Turkish conflict and ensured a lasting peace in a relative volatile area. Although it violated individual rights, it ensured the survivability of those same individuals. As the delegates negotiating at Lausanne concluded, the population exchange was necessary to avoid future mass atrocities and potential genocide.[7] The term genocide and its prerequisites were unknown to the statesmen at Lausanne, but their intuition prompted an urgency to remove the Greek Orthodox Christians from Asia Minor. However much unwanted, a population exchange might at times constitute the only solution. After all, it is better to relinquish ancestral lands than be buried on them.

---

[6]Ibid.

[7]Bent, "Uprooting of Greeks in Turkey A Modern Exodus of Outcasts."

Purpose and Organization of Study

This thesis is a case study of the 1923 Greco-Turkish population exchange that asserts the compulsory expulsion effectively prevented genocide of Orthodox Christians living in Asia Minor. To support this argument historical evidence leading up to the exchange is presented and examined for specific genocide indicators. Contemporary terms and viewpoints of genocide and mass atrocities are used to assess the historical facts and support the hypothesis. The study further addresses the exchange's long-term results. This study is focused only on the events that support the thesis and does not examine wider sociological and historical context. It is by no means a comprehensive history of Greece and Turkey following WWI. Furthermore, it does not attempt to examine the logistics of the exchange but provides a broad understanding of the process.

Chapter 2 introduces the Turkish historical background following WWI leading up to the population exchange. The narrative is focused around Mustafa Kemal Atatürk. This is done intentionally to juxtapose the Greek and Turkish leadership of the time and demonstrate the importance of individual powerful figures in times of crises. The chapter provides insight in the geopolitical events that followed WWI and the Allies attempt to dismantle the Ottoman Empire. Furthermore, the Armistices of Mudros and Treaty of Sèvres along with several other treaties are described in this chapter. Lastly, the formation of a modern nation by the victorious Mustafa Kemal Atatürk is illustrated in chapter 2. The objective of this chapter is to elucidate the Turkish perspective and the nation's road to war with Greece.

Chapter 3 describes the historical events in Greece during the tenure of Eleftherios Venizelos, an irredentist prime minister. In fact, much of the narrative is

5

focused around Venizelos, as he was in office from 1910 to 1920 and again from 1928 to 1932. The chapter also describes national territorial aspirations and the "Great Idea," a Greek irredentist philosophy. The term irredentism is defined and illustrated in the context of the Greco-Turkish war. The chapter further discusses the international support that spurred the nation's territorial aspirations leading to several regional conflicts and culminating with the Greco-Turkish War. The chapter elaborates on the circumstances that led to Greece's defeat to include the "National Schism." The National Schism along with its deleterious effect on the Asia Minor Campaign is addressed here. The objective of this chapter is to illustrate the Greek perspective and the nation's road to war with Turkey.

Chapter 4 examines the Battle of Smyrna. It describes in detail the atrocities committed by both nations in this definitive battle of the Greco-Turkish War. Thematically, the narrative of the two nations comes together in chapter 4 with tragic results. Simultaneously the stance of the international community is described as many nations have firsthand accounts of the atrocities committed. The chapter paints a clear picture of the animosity between the two nations and the resulting aftermath. Most importantly, it demonstrates a threat beyond simple conflict and the necessity for international intervention. The purpose of this chapter is to illustrate the two nation's enmity and the calamitous conflict outcomes that extended beyond reasonable animosity.

Chapter 5 is an appraisal of the Greco-Turkish War and the overall pre-existing Ottoman and Turkish attitudes towards minorities. Contemporary genocide perspectives and definitions are used to support the thesis hypothesis and secondary questions. The term genocide is defined and Gregory Stanton's eight stages of genocide are introduced

6

to support the thesis. In addition, the Armenian Genocide along with the Pontic Greek annihilation are described to further substantiate the case of potential genocide. Several firsthand accounts from western sources are used in this chapter to implicate the Turkish government's culpability in the Armenian-Pontic Genocide. The chapter's objective is to assert and support that the population exchange prevented genocide of the Greek Orthodox Christian minorities in Turkey.

Chapter 6 summarizes the events of the population exchange. It examines the economic, political, and cultural implications of the exchange on both countries. The chapter further describes why the political leaders of the time believed the population exchange was essential. Several primary sources are used to explain the reasons politicians at the time viewed the population exchange as a necessity to mitigate or stave a much worse fate for the Greek Orthodox Christians of Turkey. The Convention Concerning the Exchange of Greek and Turkish Populations and Protocol are briefly described to provide an overview of the exchange process. The chapter's objective is to illustrate the aftermath of the population exchange and to demonstrate that the statesmen of the time, after exhausting all other possibilities, believed it to be a necessity.

Chapter 7 summarizes the thesis and includes implications for current leaders.

Review of Major Literature

The historical events leading up to the population exchange are extensively documented as WWI immediately preceded, and to a point, contributed to the exchange. Several historical texts and primary sources are used to provide insight on the historical background of the two nations before the Greco-Turkish War. The sources provide primarily western perspective and therefore objectivity is assumed. A great primary source is Robert Lansing's *The Big four and Others at the Peace Conference*. Lansing

served as the U.S. Legal Advisor to the State Department during World War I and was a

member of the American Commission during the 1919 Paris Peace Conference. The

debate at the conference between the victorious Allies and the defeated Central Powers

laid the foundation for the following Greco-Turkish War. Lansing provides a candid

description of all the members gathered at the 1919 Paris Peace Conference.[8]

Several other resources provide insight in the relationship between Turkey and

Greece along with other important stories. One of the most referenced books on the

destruction of Smyrna is *The Blight of Asia: An account of the systematic extermination

of Christian populations by Mohammedans and of the culpability of certain great

powers; with a true story of the burning of Smyrna.* The book is authored by George

Horton, U.S. Consul General to Smyrna, who witnessed the destruction of Smyrna and

the associated atrocities.[9] Horton's account is commonly quoted yet his deep

religiousness adds doubt to his objectivity. A more contemporary account of the Greco-

Turkish conflict and the culminating battle at Smyrna comes from Marjorie Housepian

Dobkin's book titled *Smyrna 1922: The Destruction of a City.* Dobkin combines

interviews and historical research in her telling of the story. However, the author's

Armenian ancestry might bias her perspective.[10]

---

[8]Robert Lansing, *The Big Four and Others of the Peace Conference* (1921; repr., Cornell University Library, 2009).

[9]George Horton, *The Blight of Asia: An account of the systematic extermination of Christian populations by Mohammedans and of the culpability of certain great powers; With a true story of the burning of Smyrna* (Indianapolis: Bobbs-Merrill, 1926).

[10]Marjorie Housepian Dobkin, *Smyrna 1922 The Destruction of a City* (New York: Newmark Press, 1998).

A rather recent publication on the Greco-Turkish War and the burning of Smyrna is Giles Milton's *Paradise Lost: Smyrna, 1922.* The source material for this book includes unpublished letters and diaries written by Levantine authors residing in Smyrna. Although Milton's book does not introduce significantly new material, it is possibly one of the most unbiased accounts of the events leading up to the destruction of Smyrna. Furthermore, Milton's account corroborates events that are found in Dobkin's book.[11] Most importantly, both books are overwhelmingly supported by newspaper articles. Since WWI had just ended and negotiations were taking place, Europe was swarming with reporters covering the peace talks. The ongoing hostilities between Greece and Turkey offered great headlines to the overall world lull.

Ernest Hemingway was one such journalist covering the events in Europe. Working for the *Toronto Daily Star* he was dispatched to report on the Greco-Turkish War. He later incorporated eyewitness accounts in his collection of short stories titled, *In Our Time*. In addition, *Dateline: Toronto* is a compilation of all 172 articles written by Hemingway for the *Toronto Star*. The articles were written between 1920 and 1924 and provide great insight to the events of the time.[12] Much of Hemingway's stories are also supported by articles from other newspapers to include *The New York Times*. Edwin H. James was a reporter for *The New York Times* reporting from Paris during the Lausanne Treaty. James' articles are instrumental at describing the feelings and attitudes of the political leaders of the time.

---

[11]Giles Milton, *Paradise Lost: Smyrna 1922: The Destruction of a Christian City in the Islamic World* (New York: Basic Books, 2008).

[12]Ernest Hemingway, *Dateline: Toronto: Hemingway's Complete Toronto Star Dispatches 1920-1924* (New York: Charles Scribner's Sons, 1985).

Contemporary scholarly work on genocide was used to support the hypothesis. Invaluable are Gregory H. Stanton's *The Eight Stages of Genocide, First Working Paper* and Samantha Power's *A Problem from Hell*. Stanton is the President of Genocide Watch an organization whose purpose is to predict, prevent, stop, and punish genocide and other atrocities. He is also a Research Professor in Genocide Studies and Prevention at the Institute for Conflict Analysis and Resolution of George Mason University in Arlington, Virginia.[13] Power's award winning book offers great contemporary insight on past acts of genocide.[14] Instrumental to the support of this thesis was Taner Akcam's *A Shameful Act*. Akcam researched court records, parliamentary minutes, letters, and eyewitness accounts to support his case of an Armenian Genocide. Furthermore, *A Shameful Act* provides great insight on the attitudes of the Ottoman's towards Christian minorities.[15]

Lastly, the population exchange itself has been studied by several contemporary sources. One of the most important is *Crossing the Aegean: An Appraisal of the 1923 Compulsory Population Exchange between Greece and Turkey* by Renee Hirschon. This book is a collection of articles written by twelve different scholars. The authors have a variety of backgrounds and ethnicities including professors and researchers. The numerous articles provided a uniquely objective appraisal of the population exchange.[16]

---

[13]Gregory H. Stanton, *The Eight Stages of Genocide* (Washington, DC: Genocide Watch, 1998).

[14]Samantha Power, *A Problem from Hell: America and the Age of Genocide* (New York: Harper Perennial, 2003).

[15]Taner Akcam, *A Shameful Act: The Armenian Genocide and the Question of Turkish Responsibility* (New York: Holt Paperbacks, 2006).

[16]Hirschon, *Crossing the Aegean.*

Also important is Bruce Clark's *Twice a Stranger: The Mass Expulsions that Forged Modern Greece and Turkey.* Clark is the international security editor of *The Economist*. The book weaves together personal interviews of witnesses along with other documents and accounts of the time to illustrate both the diplomatic and human story of the exchange.[17]

---

[17]Bruce Clark, *Twice a Stranger: The mass expulsions that Forged Modern Greece and Turkey* (Cambridge: Harvard University Press, 2006).

CHAPTER 2

TURKISH PERSPECTIVE

> Heroes who shed their blood and lost their lives! You are now lying in the soil of a friendly country. Therefore rest in peace. There is no difference between the Johnnies and Mehmets to us where they lie side by side here in this country of ours. You, the mothers, who sent their sons from far away countries wipe away your tears; your sons are now lying in our bosom and are in peace. After having lost their lives on this land they have become our sons as well.
>
> — Inscribed on the Atatürk Memorial at Gallipoli

Following WWI, the Ottoman Empire was defeated along with Germany. Little hope existed for the Empire's future with its armies disarmed and its lands divided among the victors. Under such circumstances, Mustafa Kemal Atatürk, a charismatic general launched the Turkish War of Independence and implemented sweeping reforms that formed the modern nation of Turkey. While much attention during the interwar period focused on the innovation and asymmetrical development of the major military powers, Mustafa Kemal miraculously unified a collapsing country, defeated its enemies and established new national boundaries. His military achievements, however, are only surpassed by the unparalleled social and political transformations. Nevertheless, it was in the military, that Atatürk first gained fame during the Gallipoli Campaign of 1915.

At Gallipoli, 34 year-old Lieutenant Colonel Mustafa Kemal commanded the 19th Division, initially designated as the reserve forces held to the south of Gallipoli. Based on his own intuition and initiative, Kemal, moved his forces to defend Kocacimen Hill. Atatürk's gamble spoiled a British and allied attack, preventing the capture of key terrain, a pivotal point in the Gallipoli Battle. Following this success, newly promoted Colonel Kemal was appointed commander of seven divisions and conclusively defeated the Allies at Gallipoli.[18] It is also during the ensuing bloody battle for Kocacimen Hill that Mustafa

Kemal gave his famous order to the 57th Regiment: "I don't order you to attack; I order

you to die. In the time it takes us to die, other troops and commanders can come and take

our places."[19] His own willingness to die spurred his troops and catapulted Atatürk to

legendary status. For Turkey and all the nations involved, the battle had profound lasting

results. Gallipoli was viewed as the final act for the crumbling Ottoman Empire. This

success, under the leadership of Atatürk, catalyzed the Turkish War of Independence.

Despite Atatürk's accomplishment in Gallipoli and other military conflicts, the

Ottoman Empire was eventually defeated, its armies disbanded and the land divided by

the Allies, leaving only a thin slice to the Turks (figure 1). Officially, hostilities ended on

30 October 1918 with the Armistice of Mudros. Under the armistice, the Allies would

occupy the Straits of the Dardanelles and the Bosporus and be further endowed with the

right to occupy any territory to eliminate any threat to security.[20] Despite the Triple

Entente's repeated contrary statements, their intentions from the beginning of the war

were to dismantle the Ottoman Empire and to partition its land among the victorious

Allies.

---

[18]Necip Torumtay, *Ataturk* (Ankara: Turkiye Cumhuriyeti Genelkurmay
Ba'skanli gi Basimevi, 1981), 5.

[19]Ibid.

[20]A. Afetinan, *A History of the Turkish Revolution and Turkish Republic* (Ankara,
Turkey, 1981), 21.

Photo Removed Due to Copyright Restrictions

Figure 1.   Treaty of Sèvres Map

Source: Treaty of Sèvres Map, http://upload.wikimedia.org/wikipedia/commons/
a/a0/TreatyOfSèvres_%28corrected%29.PNG (accessed 8 May 2012).

In order to achieve their ultimate goals, the Allies manipulated the Greeks to

pressure the Sultan into signing another treaty. The Treaty of Sèvres, the Allies hoped

would effectively apportioned Ottoman lands to the victors, as originally planned. While

the Sultan was capitulating, the dismayed Mustafa Kemal was initiating the Turkish

National Struggle. With the help of a few friends in key positions, Kemal was appointed

to an Army Inspector's post in Anatolia, where two army corps remained.[21] On

4 September 1919, Kemal was elected the delegation head of representatives by

---

[21]Geoffrey L. Lewis, *Modern Turkey* (New York: Praeger, 1974), 69.

14

provincial delegates at the 2nd Congress thus signaling a unified resistance under his leadership.[22] Atatürk took immediate action and poised his troops to regain lost lands. Addressing smaller threats at first, Kemal effectively gained momentum and strength to achieve his ultimate goal of expelling the Greeks from Western Anatolia (Asia Minor).

Asia Minor was once brimming with wealthy ancient Greek colonies prior to Ottoman conquest, therefore, Greece coveted this land. Yet at the onset of WWI, Greece was poor, war-weary, and reluctant to get involved in any conflict.[23] After all, Greece had gained its independence in 1830, after 400 years of Ottoman rule. The repeated requests of the Triple Entente, particularly British Prime Minister David Lloyd George, convinced Greece to enter the war. In exchange for military support, Greece was promised territorial gains at the Ottoman Empire's expense.[24] Although promises were contradictory at times, overall, Greece was assured territory in areas with significant Greek populations and provenance such as Eastern Thrace and parts of western Asia Minor including the city of Smyrna (modern day Izmir).[25]

On 15 May 1919, with the cessation of hostilities and under the pretext of the Armistice of Mudros, Greek troops started pouring into Smyrna. In the eyes of the Greeks, Asia Minor belonged to them thousands of years before the Ottoman conquest and was, therefore, rightfully theirs. The Turks argued, the land was most recently

---

[22]Ibid., 71.

[23]Glenn E. Curtis, ed., Federal Research Division Library of Congress, producer, *Greece: A Country Study,* 4th ed. (Washington, DC: Department of the Army, 1995), 47.

[24]Ibid., 49.

[25]Harry N. Howard, *The Partition of Turkey: A Diplomatic History, 1913-1923* (Norman, OK: University of Oklahoma Press, 1931), 148-152.

conquered and dominated by the Ottomans for nearly 600 years. British, French and Italian troops quickly occupied the surrounding lands around Smyrna protecting the Greek flanks. Twenty thousand Greek troops with the protection of French and British navies then poured into Smyrna with little resistance. Greek forces consolidated and regrouped for the remainder of the year along the Aegean coast of modern day Turkey. Finally, in the summer of 1920, the Greek Army initiated a series of offensive operations inland with the intent of providing depth to the defense of Smyrna and, per the request of the British Prime Minister, pressure the Turkish and Ottoman governments to sign the Treaty of Sèvres.

The Sultan succumbed to foreign pressure and signed the Treaty of Sèvres on 10 August 1920. Mustafa Kemal, refusing to surrender, denounced the puppet Ottoman government and returned his uniform and honors in dismay. On 23 April 1920, Mustafa Kemal called the Grand National Assembly in Ankara and effectively formed a unified government. The Ottoman Empire, which had existed since 1299, was now officially over. Most importantly, Atatürk and his supporters, the Kemalists, were preparing to reclaim lost lands. Since the coastal area was filled with foreign troops, supported by their navies, Kemal initially concentrated his efforts inland attempting to resolve conflicts and possibly gain support from the Russians. The Bolsheviks quickly embraced Atatürk as they viewed the future Turkish Republic as a communist ally and buffer state. As history later proved, Kemal's staunch opposition to communism successfully played on the Bolsheviks expectations to garner support.

Kemal first manipulated the Bolsheviks to support his war against Armenia. As with other Ottoman lands, parts of the eastern territories were apportioned to the newly formed Democratic Republic of Armenia. The Bolsheviks were displeased as Russia now shared a border with a western ally. Quick to capitalize on the Bolsheviks anti-western sentiment, Atatürk joined forces with Russia to fight against the Armenians. On 26 April 1920, Kemal sent a message to Vladimir Lenin, the Bolsheviks leader, promising Turkish support in return for five million lira in gold and armaments. In response, Turkish forces received rifles, ammunition to include artillery shells and 200.6 kg of gold bullion. Armenians were similarly supported by Allied forces, poised to defend against a Turkish attack.

Turkish forces eventually defeated the Armenian forces within four months. Hostilities officially ceased on 18 November 1920 and the two nations signed the Treaty of Alexandropol on 2 December. The treaty called for Armenia to disarm most of its military, cede over 50 percent of its pre-war territory and relinquish all territories granted by the Treaty of Sèvres. Ratification of the Treaty of Alexandropol was halted, however, when Bolsheviks forces entered the Armenian capital of Yerevan on 4 December 1920. The duplicitous Bolshevik government, while supporting the invading Turkish forces, also signed a Soviet-Armenian agreement, promising Russian support specifically in securing Yerevan. With Soviet forces now securing the Armenian capital city, the Turks had to draft another agreement, the Treaty of Kars, to satisfy all nations involved.

The Treaty of Kars was ratified by the representatives of Soviet Azerbaijan, Soviet Armenian, Soviet Georgian, and the Grand National Assembly of Turkey. The Soviets were very satisfied with the outcomes of the Armenian war that led to an outpouring of support for the Kemalist and the ongoing war effort to liberate Turkey and expel the Allied forces. Armenia although no longer an independent state, was glad to be

17

under Soviet rule instead of Turkish. A great deal of animosity existed between the two nations throughout history and the treaty offered a short reprieve from hostilities.

With the Treaty of Kars, Atatürk stabilized the interior and eastern fronts and could now focus all his attention and resources combating the Greeks. Most importantly, Turkish forces now had the support of Russia.[26] At the same time, sensing a shift in favor for the Kemalist, the French and Italians both made private agreements with the Turks. Thus, Greece a nation that in part was convinced by France and Italy to join the Triple Entente was now betrayed by those same nations. In fact, France and Italy both sold arms to the Kemalist and the Italians even used their base in Antalya to gather intelligence on the Greeks and convey that information to the Turks. Britain was the only nation still supporting the Greeks but eventually that support languished. With such circumstances, the Turks effectively halted the Greeks and quickly repelled them back into the coastal area.

As a last resort early in 1922, Greece appealed to Britain, France and Italy for support. The Allies, who viewed the Treaty of Sèvres as unenforceable, refused to support them. France and Italy then signed individual treaties with the Turkish Revolutionaries, removing all their troops and leaving the Greek soldiers exposed. Finally, the allied forces proposed an armistice in March 1922. Mustafa Kemal, however, realized he now had the military advantage and refuse any settlements while Greek forces remained in Asia Minor.[27] Gathering momentum, Atatürk reorganized his troops and

---

[26]Afetinan, *A History of the Turkish Revolution and Turkish Republic*, 96.

[27]Richard Clogg, *A Concise History of Greece* (Cambridge: Cambridge University Press, 1992), 95.

18

started a counter-offensive to expel the Greeks. With the logistics lines severed and their flanks exposed, Greek forces stood no chance against the well-equipped and Russian supported Turkish forces. Within six months, Atatürk expelled all foreign forces and reclaimed Smyrna, a bastion of Greek culture and civilization, for Turkey.

Uncontested, Mustafa Kemal changed the tide of war. His military brilliance was paralleled only by his political genius. Kemal manipulated Bolsheviks, enticed nationalists, and placated religious leaders galvanizing all factions towards his goal of Turkish liberation. Regardless of his monumental military victories, his greatest achievements were yet to come. Mustafa Kemal, with unprecedented sweeping reforms, transformed the remnants of an Islamic empire into a modern republic. He standardized and advocated education, supported women's rights, separated politics and religion, promoted art and culture and even introduced a new alphabet to facilitate reading. Never in history has one person affected his country so significantly. It is no surprise then, that Mustafa Kemal in 1934 received by his countrymen the legal surname of Atatürk, Turkish for father of Turks.[28]

---

[28]Sir Harry Luke, *The Old Turkey and the New, from Byzantium to Ankara* (London: Bles, 1955), 219.

CHAPTER 3

GREEK PERSPECTIVE

The Greek kingdom is not the whole of Greece, but only a part, the smallest and poorest part. A native is not only someone who lives within the Kingdom, but also one who lives in Ioannina, in Thessaly, in Serres, in Adrianople, in Constantinople, in Trebizoid, in Crete, in Samos and in any land associated with Greek history or the Greek race. . . . There are two main centres of Hellenism: Athens, the capital of the Greek kingdom, (and) 'The City' (Constantinople), the dream and hope of all Greeks.[29]

— Ioannis Kolettis before the constituent assembly in 1844

Photo Removed Due to Copyright Restrictions

Figure 2.   Map of Greece's Expansion 1832 1947

Source: Greece Maps, http://mapsof.net/map/map-of-greece-expansion-1832-1947 (accessed 29 February 2012).

---

[29]Clogg, *A Concise History of Greece*, 47.

Ioannis Kolettis, Greek Prime Minister from 1844 to 1847, conceived the "Megali Idea," translated to "Great Idea." This great idea was an irredentist philosophy of nationalism that envisioned the establishment of a state encompassing all ethnic Greek inhabited areas. Unification of these populated lands became the core of foreign policy from the nation's 1830 Ottoman independence until the early 20th century. Following its independence, Greece encompassed only a fraction of the lands of the modern nation. Since a large number of Greeks remained under Ottoman rule, realization of the Great Idea guaranteed popular support and success for any politician who pursued it. This pervasive nationalism eventually peaked during Eleftherios Venizelos' tenure as Prime Minister from 1910 to 1920 and again from 1928 to 1932. With Venizelos at the reins, Greece doubled in population and area and came close to accomplishing the Great Idea.[30]

Eleftherios Venizelos first gained popularity as a staunch advocate for the unification of Crete with mainland Greece. While parts of the mainland gained independence from the Ottomans in 1821, Crete remained under Turkish control. Crete is a large island south of the mainland. The island was home to the Minoans, Europe's first advanced civilization. Since antiquity, the island is known for its beauty, civilization and its bellicose inhabitants. Remaining true to their nature, Cretans resisted Ottoman rule unlike other parts of Greece. While most of Greece was occupied for 400 years, Crete's occupation lasted 200 years. During the two centuries of Turkish rule Cretans persistently revolted, resulting in large number of casualties on both sides. The pervasive clashes fomented the enmity of the two. Unquestionably, Venizelos' Cretan descent greatly

---

[30]Ibid., 46-48.

affected the politician's temperament and Greece's stance during his tenure as Prime Minister.[31]

Like his ancestors, Venizelos revolted against Ottoman rule, clamoring for unification with Greece. In 1897 during a specific uprising, Ottoman troops massacred a large number of Christians in retaliation. Pressured by public opinion, the nascent Greek government sent troops to defend the Cretans. In response to its involvement, the Great Powers (Britain, France, Russia, and Italy) were forced to intervene in order to uphold the Pact of Halepa. The pact was an agreement between the Ottoman Empire and the Great Powers, attempting to keep unrest in Crete from spilling over to the rest of Europe. According to the agreement, Crete became a semi-independent state within the Ottoman Empire. When the European powers attempted to enforce the pact, they were dismayed to discover the landing of Greek troops on Crete had initiated an uprising, which spread throughout the island. In retaliation to Greece's interference, the European warships blockaded Crete and landed troops to prevent the Greek army from approaching the capital of Hania.[32]

Venizelos noticed Hania in flames and immediately headed towards the city. En route, he came across Cretan rebels and after a short conversation, agreed to lead them. A persuasive leader, Venizelos convinced the Cretan rebels to attack a promontory on the northern side of the island called Akrotiri. He and the rebels successfully displaced Turkish forces at Akrotiri and spent the night there, defiantly raising a Greek flag.

---

[31]Andrew Dalby, *Eleftherios Venizelos: Greece* (London: Haus Publishing, 2010), 3-17.

[32]Ibid.

Infuriated by the flag raising the Ottoman forces requested support from the Great

Powers' warships, which in response, bombarded the rebel positions. The Cretan

politician then wrote a letter to the European admirals protesting the shelling and

deliberately leaked it to international newspapers. European citizens were outraged to

hear their forces were attacking fellow Christians. Venizelos' letter further spurred

support for Crete's struggle from European nations and their citizens. Eventually, the

Great Powers yielded to public opinion and declared Crete an autonomous state under

Ottoman suzerainty. This autonomy was short lived. Continuous unrest resulted in the

Great Powers eventually assigning the King of Greece the authority to appoint the

island's leadership. This move effectively nullified Ottoman suzerainty and transferred

authority to Greece.[33]

Venizelos' instrumental role in Crete's overthrow of Ottoman rule, along with his

actions at Akrotiri, elevated him to legendary status in Greek folklore and politics. In

May 1909, he was invited to lead a group of military officers that wanted to reform the

national government and reorganize the army.[34] In 1910, he successfully implemented

political improvements, which in turn, resulted in his election as Prime Minister.

Immediately upon taking office, he started a series of economic and political reforms that

proved instrumental in Greece's future success. While revitalizing the economy and

society, the prime minister simultaneously significantly strengthened the military. A

---

[33]Ibid.

[34]M. Mazower, "The messiah and the bourgeoisie: Venizelos and politics in Greece, 1909- 1912," *The Historical Journal* 35, no. 4 (1992): 885-904.

nationalist at heart, he knew strong military forces could be required to extend Greece's territory.[35]

Working towards the irredentist philosophy, Venizelos started taking actions to achieve the Great Idea. Well aware his military was too weak to take on Turkish forces alone, he formed an alliance with Serbia, Bulgaria and Montenegro. In 1912, the alliance, known as the Balkan League, went to war with Turkey. The First Balkan War substantiated Venizelos' strong investments in the military. Greek naval forces occupied islands and successfully prevented any Turkish reinforcements. Simultaneously, the army expanded territorial gains northeast of Athens, buffered by their naval supremacy in the Aegean Sea.[36]

Venizelos' contributions to the First Balkan War were by all accounts immeasurable. In a 1921 article titled "Venizelos, Maker of Modern Greece" the politician is praised once more for his political prudence. Journalist J.W. Duffield stated the following about Venizelos during the Balkan Wars:

> The Balkan wars of 1912-1913 made Venizelos a world figure. It was his consummate statesmanship that welded the discordant little States of Greece, Bulgaria, Serbia and Montenegro into a compact mass that hurled itself on Turkey with vigor and momentum before which the Sultan's forces crumpled like paper.[37]

Although the First Balkan War was a resounding success for Greek forces, it divided the country politically due to quarreling between the prime minister and

---

[35]Clogg, *A Concise History of* Greece, 71-77.

[36]Ibid., 77-81.

[37]J. W. Duffield, "Venizelos, Maker of Modern Greece," *The New York Times,* 30 October 1921.

country's prince. The first point of contention arose from the irregular chain of command. Venizelos as prime minister of Greece was in charge of the Ministry of Defense, which had overall control of the military. Therefore, Prince Constantine, as the army commander, was subordinate to Venizelos, but as future King of Greece was superior to the Prime Minister. Thus, the chain of command of the military was disjointed and further exacerbated by the strained relationship between the two. Venizelos and the Prince continuously quarreled over military and political objectives. Tensions between the two eventually divided the country and resulted into what became known as the National Schism.[38]

However, the two men put aside their animosity to focus on the Second Balkan War. Venizelos' foresight had once again anticipated another Balkan war. On 19 May1913, fearing a Bulgarian threat, Greece and Serbia signed a pact alliance. The following month, on 19 June 1913, Bulgaria initiated the Second Balkan War with a surprise attack on both Greece and Serbia. Constantine, now King, successfully led the army repelling the Bulgarians. On 28 June 1913, overwhelmed by Serbian and Greek military successes, Bulgaria capitulated and signed a peace treaty. While Venizelos' political forethought forged essential alliances, King Constantine skillfully led his army to victory. By the end of the Balkan Wars, the two men had effectively doubled Greece in population and territory. However, the next war, WWI, would further distance Venizelos from the King, increasing the National Schism.[39]

---

[38]Dalby, *Eleftherios Venizelos: Greece*, 55-75.

[39]Frank Smothers, William Hardy McNeill, and Elizabeth Darbishire McNeill, *Report on the Greeks: Findings of a Twentieth Century Fund team which surveyed conditions in Greece in 1947* (New York: The Twentieth Century Fund, 1948).

With the onset of WWI, Greece initially remained neutral while the Prime Minister and the King argued which side to join. King Constantine favored the Central Powers as his wife, Queen Sophia was German. In addition to being the German Emperor's brother-in-law, Constantine received his military training in Germany and believed in the German military's superiority. Venizelos, on the other hand, sided with the Triple Entente. Since Greece was a seafaring nation and comprised of several islands, he feared French and English naval control of the Mediterranean, if opposed, could be detrimental to his country. Thus in 1915 when Winston Churchill offered Greece the opportunity to participate in the allied Dardanelles Campaign, Venizelos was eager to comply. King Constantine, however, disagreed and the irate Prime Minister resigned. Although Venizelos quit his office at the time, his political career continued and he once again won the elections that followed.[40]

Following Venizelos' reelection, the two continued to bicker. King Constantine eventually forced the Prime Minister to resign a second time and dissolved the Parliament calling for new elections. Finding the monarch's actions unconstitutional, Venizelos refused to run for reelection. With Venizelos' departure, the Allies now feared Greece would form an alliance with the Central Powers. Furthermore, on 26 May 1916, Greece unconditionally surrendered Fort Rupel in Macedonia to German and Bulgarian forces. Its surrender both angered and worried the Allies. Allied forces withdrawing from Gallipoli had amassed in the city of Salonika dangerously near Fort Rupel. Exploiting Greece's lack of means to resist and attempts to remain neutral, Greek sovereignty was often violated by both sides during WWI. In addition, the surrender angered those loyal

---

[40]Curtis.

26

to Venizelos, which feared Bulgarian territorial claims of northern Greek lands. Accordingly, Bulgarians started displacing Greek citizens in northern Greece by September of 1916. Bulgaria's territorial aspirations eventually culminated with the occupation of the northern Greek city Kavala.[41]

Angered at Constantine's actions and Bulgarian occupation of Greek territory, Venizelos organized a coup effectively splitting the country in two. On 9 October 1916, with the support of the Allied troops in Salonika, Venizelos along with two Greek military officers established the Provisional Government of National Defense. The provisional state based in the northern Greek city of Salonika included the new lands gained during the Balkan Wars. Uninhibited, Venizelos and his supporters (called Venizelist) immediately raised a military in Macedonia to fight the Central Powers and regain lost territory. On 2 December 1916, Britain and France officially recognized the Venizelos' government as the lawful government, effectively splitting the nation in two. Fearing further escalation, France and Great Britain imposed a naval embargo on southern Greece offering to raise it only if the king resigned. On 15 June 1917, Constantine abdicated, went into exile, and left his younger son, the pro-Allied Alexander on the throne.[42]

With Alexander on the throne Venizelos returned to a now unified, but not politically united, Greece that officially entered the war on the side of the Allies. Royalists were angered at Constantine's exile and foreign power meddling in the nation's internal politics. With the nation still polarized, by 1918, the entire Greek army was

---

[41]Clogg, *A Concise History of Greece*, 87.

[42]Dalby, *Eleftherios Venizelos: Greece*, 80.

27

mobilized fighting against the Central Powers in Macedonia. Under the command of a French general, a combined Greek, Serbian, French and British force initiated offensive operations against the Germans and Bulgarians. First Bulgaria, once defeated, signed an armistice and soon Hungary followed. In November 1918, Hungary officially surrendered which dissolved the Austro-Hungarian Empire. Hungary's surrender also catalyzed the end of WWI, as Germany had no forces to defend against an Allied attack from the south. Thus, with the support of the Greek Military, Allied forces broke the Macedonian front and defeated the Hungarians, a decisive event in WWI.[43]

Following Greece's contributions to the Macedonian front, the nation was greatly rewarded in the ensuing peace talks. Greek troops, numbering over 300,000 comprised the largest force by a single nation in the Macedonia front. Without a doubt, Greece's contribution of fresh troops significantly benefited the Allies at a decisive moment. As a result, Venizelos earned a seat at the 1919 Paris Peace Conference. The Greek Prime Minister's influential role in Paris is well document by Robert Lansing. Lansing served as the U.S. Legal Advisor to the State Department during WWI and was a member of the American Commission during the peace conference. In 1921, he published *The Big Four and Others at the Peace Conference*. In his book, Lansing provides a candid description of all the members gathered at the 1919 Paris Peace Conference. On Venizelos, Lansing wrote the following:

> No man who attended the Peace Conference aroused more general interest because of the part that he had played in the war or won more friends because of his personality than did Eleftherios Venizelos. . . .

---

[43]Robert Bideleux and Ian Jeffries, *A History of Eastern Europe: Crisis and Change* (New York: Routledge, 2007), 127.

The views of M. Venizelos were, I believe, given greater weight by the Big Four than those of any other single delegate at Paris, while the confidence which he inspired made less difficult his task of obtaining the terms which he desired to have inserted in the treaties with Turkey and with Bulgaria.

Except for the personal influence of M. Venizelos, I am convinced that the extension of Greek sovereignty would not have been so great as it was under the treaties. What he asked was granted because *he* asked it.[44]

Evidently, according to Lansing, the Greek Prime Minister's political acumen was instrumental during the peace conference, resulting in significant Greek territorial gains at the expense of mostly Turkey and Bulgaria. Almost overnight, Greece acquired Western Thrace, Eastern Thrace, Smyrna, Imvros, Tenedos and the Dodecanese except Rhodes. The politician's effective role during the Paris Peace Conference and the ensuing treaties made him very popular among his countrymen. Nevertheless, Greece was still polarized between Venizelist and pro-royalist. The conflict peaked with an assassination attempt of Venizelos by two pro-royalist soldiers in Paris. Although the assassination failed, the event caused great unrest in Greece, where he was now revered by most citizens.[45]

Once he recovered, Venizelos was welcomed back to Greece as a national hero, but the jubilant atmosphere was short lived. The Armistice of Mudros, ended hostilities between the Allies and the Ottoman Empire following WWI. Despite the Triple Entente's repeated contrary statements, their intentions from the beginning were to dismantle the Ottoman Empire and partition its land among the victorious Allies. Thus, the Allies used the pretext of the armistice and the Greek military, to achieve their true intentions. As

---

[44]Lansing, *The Big Four and Others of the Peace Conference*, 142.

[45]"Venizelos Shot, Twice Wounded by Greeks in Paris," *The New York Times*, 13 August 1920.

part of the Mudros Armistice, the Allies were authorized to occupy certain Ottoman lands. Consequently, 20,000 Greek troops poured with little resistance into Smyrna on 15 May 1919. In the summer of 1920, the Greek Army initiated a series of offensive operations inland with the intent of providing depth to the defense of Smyrna and, per the request of the British Prime Minister, pressure the Turkish and Ottoman governments to sign the Treaty of Sèvres. On 10 August 1920, the Sultan succumbed to foreign pressure and signed the Treaty of Sèvres.[46]

The Treaty of Sèvres effectively apportioned Ottoman lands to the Allies although the treaty was never completely achieved. According to the treaty, Turkey ceded eastern Thrace and Smyrna to Greece. Unbeknownst to the Turks, this had been decided over a year ago in the Paris Peace Talks. The excessively cruel Greek offensive operations had the reverse effect of what the Allies intended and started the Turkish War of Independence. Under the leadership of Mustafa Kemal Atatürk, the Turkish liberation movement repelled Greek forces and quickly squashed any Allied territorial aspirations. Britain, France and Italy made private agreements with Atatürk, withdrawing their troops and turning their backs on the Greeks. With their flanks exposed and lacking logistical support from the Allies, Greek troops were defeated. The Allies, which had convinced the Greek military to initiate the offensive operations, now used a reemerging political turmoil in Greece as a pretext to sever all ties with nation.[47]

The polarization of Greece between Venizelist and pro-royalist emerged again when King Alexander suddenly died. On 25 October 1920 just as Atatürk shifted the

---

[46]Thea Halo, *Not Even my Name* (New York: Picardo, 2001), 119-120.

[47]Ibid., 120-121.

Greco-Turkish War in his favor, Alexander died of blood poisoning from a pet monkey bite. His death brought his father, Constantine, back from exile to rein as the Greek King. The same year, Venizelos lost the election and decided to leave for Paris. The political changeover greatly angered the Great Powers who opposed Constantine's return. The Allies found the political turmoil in Greece an easy pretext to halt Greek military support. In reality, the Allies viewed the Treaty of Sèvres as unenforceable. Hastily, France and Italy signed individual treaties with the Turkish Revolutionaries, removing all their troops and leaving the Greek soldiers exposed.[48]

Nevertheless, the greatest damage to the Asia Minor Campaign came from within Greece. Once the pro-royalist government came to power, they decided to continue the Asia Minor Campaign. In an act of defiance, the new government foolishly dismissed all the pro-Venizelist experienced military officers. The new government further continued to purge the military for petty reasons that were viewed as dissent.[49] Inevitably, the new government poised the Greek forces for defeat. Without allied support, and Greece's internal bickering, Atatürk expelled Greek forces within six months and reclaimed Smyrna. Following the unexpected defeat King Constantine was once more dethroned and replaced by his eldest son, George. Venizelos was once again called upon to negotiate peace with the victorious Turks.[50]

Peace negotiations lasted an arduous eight months at a conference in Swiss city of Lausanne. On 24 July 1923, The Treaty of Lausanne recognized the sovereignty of the

---

[48]Ibid.

[49]Hemingway, *Dateline: Toronto*, location 4326.

[50]Halo, *Not Even my Name*, 120-121.

Republic of Turkey and annulled the Treaty of Sèvres. Greece surrendered eastern

Thrace, Imbros, and Tenedos back to Turkey. One of the most intriguing aspects of the

treaty was the Convention concerning the Exchange of Greek and Turkish Populations.

Signed on 30 January 1923, the convention called for the compulsory and exchange of

more than 500,000 Muslim Turks expelled from Greece and over a million Christian

Greeks expelled from Turkey.[51] Article I of the Convention states:

> As from the 1st May, 1923, there shall take place a compulsory exchange of
> Turkish national of the Greek Orthodox religion established in Turkish territory,
> and of Greek nationals of the Moslem religion established in Greek territory.
>
> These persons shall not return to live in Turkey or Greece respectively without the
> authorization of the Turkish Government or of the Greek Government
> respectively.[52]

The population exchange shaped the societies of both nations unlike any

territorial gains or military conflicts. Regardless of the long-term effects, for Venizelos

and Greece the Asia Minor Campaign and consecutive population exchange were

disastrous. What started as the near realization of the Great Idea, resulted in what today

the Greeks call the Asia Minor Catastrophe. Despite the Greek military defeat in Smyrna

and the eventual concessions towards Turkey, Venizelos political career the following

years alternated between popular support and opposition. Like a Greek tragedy, political

turmoil in his homeland resulted in Venizelos dying in 1936 while on a self-imposed

exile in Paris. History vindicated him and today he is widely considered the maker of

modern Greece. Due to his foresight and political sagacity, Greece's territory and

---

[51]Clark, *Twice a Stranger*, xi-xii.

[52]"Convention concerning the exchange of Greek and Turkish populations," *The American Journal of International Law* 18, no. 2 (1924): 84-90.

population grew with unprecedented momentum during his tenure as Prime Minister. His

countrymen, recognizing his contributions, bestowed him the title of ethnarch, meaning

leader of the nation.[53]

---

[53]Hirschon, *Crossing the Aegean*, 1-20.

CHAPTER 4

DESTRUCTION OF SYMRNA (IZMIR)

> The worst, he said, were the women with the dead babies. You couldn't get the women to give up their dead babies. They'd have babies dead for six days. Wouldn't give them up. Nothing you could do about it. Had to take them away finally.[54]
>
> — Ernest Hemingway, *On Quai at Smyrna*

On September 1922, sailors from around the world witnessed the destruction of Smyrna, a city previously known as the ornament of Asia. Twenty-one Allied warships overlooked the city but did not intervene in order to maintain neutrality. Those aboard the ships recounted their experiences to a young reporter named Ernest Hemingway. Hemingway, at the time a journalist, was dispatched to report on the Greco-Turkish War. He later incorporated the eyewitness accounts in his collection of short stories titled *In Our Time*. His collection opens with "On Quai at Smyrna."[55]

With his classic terse prose, the author purposefully brings the reader seemingly midway into a conversation. Hemingway utilizes imagery of death, suffering, animal cruelty and ends with the remarks "It was a pleasant business. My word yes a most pleasant business."[56] The author's masterful use of sarcasm and anachronism disorient and transport the reader into the mindset of a confused American Sailor witnessing the destruction of a city. Like Hemingway's story, the burning of Smyrna is obfuscated by

---

[54]Ernest Hemingway, *In Our Time* (New York: Scribner, 2002), 83.

[55]Caroline Hulse, "Ernest Hemingway," http://www.ernest.hemingway.com/ Elizabethhadley.htm (accessed 5 April 2012).

[56]Hemingway, *In Our Time*, 100-101.

contradictory statements, with both Turks and Greeks placing the blame on each other. A low moment in both nations' histories the events in Smyrna unquestionably spurred the Greco-Turkish population exchange.

In order to effectively appreciate Smyrna's destruction, the events of the short-lived three-year Greek occupation must be revisited. On 5 May 1919, according to the Armistice of Mudros, Greek forces poured into Smyrna. As a pretext to justify the landings, the Greek government claimed it was protecting its population in the area.[57] The troops were initially greeted by a jubilant crowd, which included the Orthodox Metropolitan, Chrysostomos. Turkish officers and soldiers had peacefully complied with Allied orders and were confined to their barracks. The Greeks approached the confined soldiers and started escorting them out of the barracks and out of Smyrna.[58][59]

Suddenly, a shot rang out which immediately panicked the crowd. In response, the Greek troops started firing indiscriminately while other civilians seized the opportunity to round up innocent Turkish civilians and abuse them. Once the panic subsided, the Turkish soldiers continued forcefully marching through a gauntlet of bystander insults and abuse. General Ali Nadir Pasha, the Turkish Army Corps Commander was outraged at the shootings and at the maltreatment of his men. Specifically insulting, the Greek troops made his soldiers shout, "Long live Greece, long live Venizelos" as they marched. The General reported he had lost 40 men in the panic.[60]

---

[57]Dobkin, *Smyrna 1922 The Destruction of a City*, 63.

[58]Ibid., 65.

[59]Milton, *Paradise Lost*, 162.

[60]Dobkin, *Smyrna 1922 The Destruction of a City*, 66.

It is unknown who fired the shot that incited the pandemonium resulting in Turkish military and civilian casualties. Captain John Dayton commander of the United States Battleship Arizona claimed the shots came from a Turkish concealed position. Other American authorities believed the shot came from a small Turkish boat anchored by the shore. Others believed it came from one of the criminals released from the prison of Smyrna the night before the Greek landing.[61] Regardless of the culprit's nationality, it was surprising to many the Allies had allowed Greek troops to occupy a volatile town with so much animosity between the two nations. U.S. Consul George Horton had anticipated many more reprisals and he attributed the violence to Greeks who had been abused in the past and had no recourse whatever but to endure.[62] Smyrna afterwards remained relatively peaceful under Greek control, despite the initial turmoil.

To establish order in the city, Prime Minister Venizelos appointed Aristidis Stergiadis as the High Commissioner of Smyrna. Stergiadis was selected because he was a stern disciplinarian and would, hopefully, prevent further outrages against the Muslim population. By all accounts, the Commissioner upheld Christian-Muslim equality, to the chagrin of the local Christians.[63] In one instance, Horton witnessed Stergiadis standing up to the Metropolitan Chrysostomos. In his book, *The Blight of Asia* wrote the following about the encounter:

> On one occasion I was present at an important service in the Orthodox Cathedral, to which the representative of the various powers, as well as the principal Greek authorities had been invited. The high-commissioner had given the order that the

---

[61]Ibid., 66-67; Milton, *Paradise Lost*, 162-164.

[62]Horton, *The Blight of Asia*, Chapter 10.

[63]Clogg, *A Short History of Modern Greece*, 114.

service should be strictly religious and non-political. Unfortunately, Archbishop Chrysostom (he who was later murdered by the Turks) began to introduce some politics into his sermon, a thing which he was extremely prone to do. Sterghiades, who was standing near him, interrupted, saying: "But I told you I didn't want any of this." The archbishop flushed, choked, and breaking off his discourse abruptly, ended with, "In the name of the Father, Son and Holy Ghost, Amen," and stepped off the rostrum.[64]

Regardless of Stergiades' administration, Smyrna's tenuous tranquility was short lived. By September 1922 the three-year Greco-Turkish War was coming to a definitive end. Greek troops, previously augmented by Allied logistics and overall support, were now completely abandoned with their flanks exposed as the Italian, British, and French withdrew their forces. Conversely, Turkish resistance under the leadership of Mustafa Kemal had mustered Italian, French, and Russian support to combat the Greeks.[65] Kemal's culminating effort for Turkish unification and independence was the expulsion of Greek forces from Smyrna. On 7 September, the eve of certain capture of the city, Mustafa Kemal sent a proclamation to the local papers that stated any Turkish soldiers molesting noncombatants of any nationality would be executed. The French and Italian consuls further appeased the crowds claiming the minorities will be in no danger from the approaching Turkish forces. Kemalist troops also distributed leaflets with Atatürk's proclamation in both Greek and Turkish.[66] The city's Christians, however, were apprehensive, as they had heard Greek troops committed atrocities during their retreat.

---

[64]Horton, *The Blight of Asia*, Chapter 10.

[65]Clogg, *A Concise History of Greece*, 95-96.

[66]Dobkin, *Smyrna 1922 The Destruction of a City*, 121; Milton, *Paradise Lost*, 273-277.

The defeated Greek forces were committing outrages during the final phase of the Greco-Turkish War. Numerous sources attest that while the Greek army was retreating, it carried out a scorched-earth policy. James Loder Park, U.S. Vice-Consul in Constantinople toured the cities surrounding Smyrna immediately after Greek troops evacuated the sites. According to Park, many of the cities were destroyed by Greeks. The Vice-Consul stated the burning and destruction were planned and organized. Park concluded that Greek atrocities of murder and torture were well in the thousands in the four cities he visited.[67] Because of the retreating troops appalling behavior, the minorities in Smyrna rightfully feared possible retaliation from the approaching Turkish forces.

On 9 September 1922, Turkish advance cavalry entered Smyrna unimpeded as Greek forces had evacuated the last of their soldiers the previous night. By all reports, the city was eerily calm for a day until on 10 September 1922 all havoc broke loose. Interestingly, Kemal on that same day sent a confusing message to the Secretary of the League of Nations. The message stated that "on account for the excited spirit of the Turkish population the Angora Government would not be responsible for massacres."[68] Kemal's message perplexed the League and it was perceived as an indication that massacres had already begun, which they had.

Turkish outrages against civilians in Smyrna were directed towards Greeks and Armenians. Jewish and Levantine (European) communities were for the most part unmolested. Atatürk either knew about the pogroms or anticipated them and that may be

---

[67]U.S. Vice-Consul James Loder Park to Secretary of State, Smyrna, 11 April 1923. US Archive US767.68116/34.

[68]Edwin L. James, "Kemal Won't Insure Against Massacres," *The New York Times*, 11 September 1922.

the reason he sent the cryptic message to the League of Nations. Perhaps he worried about Turkey's future relationship with Western nations that he undoubtedly coveted. The composition of the Turkish forces may have also been the source of Kemal's reservations. According to Turkish historian Resat Kasaba, the Turkish forces that entered Smyrna were comprised largely by armed irregulars called *efes*, *cetes*, and *zeybeks*. These armed irregulars came from diverse nefarious backgrounds including draft dodgers, bandits, tax evaders, and petty criminals. In return for their services the Kemalists, halfheartedly, allowed the bandit leaders to raid, rob and loot mostly Christians. Kasaba further asserts that without these outsiders, Izmir (Smyrna) may not have been destroyed or at least not to the extent that it was.[69]

The outsiders that Kasaba describes also included Greek troops that came from mainland Greece. These Unanlar troops, filled with nationalists' fanaticism were brutal to Turkish troops and civilians. Unanlar, Rumlar, and Karamanlilar are all Turkish words for Greeks with slight yet significant distinctions. Unanlar were Greeks that lived in mainland Greece and had no ties to Turkey. The other two terms refer to Greeks that lived in Asia Minor (Anatolia). Rumlar were primarily Greek-speaking Greeks that resided mostly near Constantinople as well on Imbros and Tenedos. Finally, Karamanlilar by all accounts, were Turkish except for their Greek Orthodox religion. Kasaba claimed the atrocities of the retreating fervent Unanlar troops spurred the Turks to retaliate indiscriminately against all Greeks and other minorities.[70]

---

[69]Dobkin, *Smyrna 1922 The Destruction of a City*, 127; Resat Kasaba, "Izmir 1922: A Port City Unravels," in *Modernity and Culture*, ed. Leila Tarazi Fawa, and C. A. Bayly (New York: Columbia University Press, 2002), 204-229.

[70]Ibid.

Kemal's cryptic message to the League of Nations, indeed, heralded a flurry of hard to believe atrocity reports from several sources. One of the first shocking accounts regarded the Greek religious leader and Greek Metropolitan, Chrysostomos. Shortly after noon on Sunday, 10 September 1922, Chrysostomos was summoned by General Noureddin. As the priest extended his hand in greeting, the general spat at him. In disgust, the general exclaimed he would not touch his filthy hand. Noureddin informed Chrysostomos he was condemned to death by a revolutionary tribunal in Angora. As the Metropolitan was escorted out of the building, Noureddin went out to the balcony and shouted to the waiting mob, "Treat him as he deserves!"

The crowd seized Chrysostomos in front of the 12 French Marines who were escorting him, and dragged the cleric to a barbershop. A white sheet was taken from the barbershop and placed around the Metropolitan's neck as the crowd shouted "Give him a shave!" Chrysostomos' beard was torn off, his eyes gouged out, and his ears, nose and hands cut off. In disbelief, the French Marines attempted to intervene, but were stopped by the officer in charge.[71] The situation quickly spiraled out of control and additional Greeks and Armenians were massacred in the ensuing frenzy. The nearby minority civilians, fearing for their lives, sought refuge with the Allied forces that were protecting various national interests in Smyrna. The following days in scenes reminiscent of Rwanda in 1993, Western troops witnessed massacre after massacre and were prohibited from intervening. American forces were in an even greater quagmire.

---

[71]Dobkin, *Smyrna 1922 The Destruction of a City*, 133-134; Milton, *Paradise Lost*, 273-277.

The U.S., initially neutral but later siding with Turkey, sent three destroyers to Smyrna. Ordered by President Warren G. Harding, the USS Litchfield was specifically sent to retrieve the body of PFC George Dilboy. A Greek-American, Dilboy was a Medal of Honor recipient. At the requests of his father, Dilboy's body was to be buried in his birthplace of Alatsata, near Smyrna. As the soldier's American flag draped casket rested in an Orthodox Church, Turkish troops seized the town and the church. Marauding troops entered the church, tore off the flag and scattered the Private's remains over the floor. When newspapers in the U.S. circulated the story, Americans were outraged. Further exacerbating the situation, the respected General John Pershing listed George Dilboy as one of the war's 10 greatest heroes. As a result, the American public demanded action. Once the Turks realized their mistakes, an honor guard delivered the casket to a U.S. landing party. Dilboy was eventually buried with full military honors at Arlington National Cemetery.[72]

On 13 September, four days after the Turkish Army entered Smyrna the city was set ablaze. Interestingly the atrocities and the fire seemed to have started in the Armenian quarter. It was the Greeks, after all, not the Armenians that occupied Smyrna. The flames and the chaos quickly spread causing people to flee towards the harbor and the 21 Allied warships. Greek and Armenian residents expected retaliation but they wrongfully believed the presence of the Allies would curtail the Turkish forces and possibly aid any refugees. Instead, claiming neutrality, international forces provided no support as they watched and listened to the victims' cries. Discipline spiraled quickly out of control, as

---

[72]Michael R. Patterson, "Arlington National Cemetery," 25 September 2000, http://www.arlingtoncemetery.net/gdilboy.htm (accessed 5 April 2012); Dobkin, *Smyrna 1922 The Destruction of a City*, 123.

Turkish soldiers brutalized by three years of war now had no repercussions for their actions. Alcohol and the jubilant mood further fomented the situation. Soon the city descended into an orgy of atrocities flagrantly committed in daylight in front of many witnesses.

Lieutenant Charles Howes, an officer aboard the King George V, looking through binoculars from the ship, was monitoring the violence on the harbor. He witnessed two young women, after being raped by Turkish soldiers, had their breasts cut off and their bodies placed in the roadway outside a British business. At the same time, the city's harbor was filling with people trying to flee from the Turks and the fire. Hundreds of thousands of homeless had converted the area into a makeshift refugee camp. The heat became so great that the ships had to move 250 yards away from the bay in fear combustible liquids on board might ignite. Some refugees holding on to the harbor sides, jumped in the water to seek reprieve from the heat. At which time, a seaman observed Turkish soldiers with a scimitar severing their arms. The mutilated bodies plummeted to their deaths into the water.[73]

Other bodies were dumped in the harbor and the current carried them towards the British fleet. A seaman serving on the HMS Serapis recalled his horror when he went to investigate a knocking noise. Peering over the rails, he noticed a body floating in the upright position repeatedly banging on the side of the ship like a buoy. Evidently, the carcass had been tied in a sack below the waist and weighted down on the bottom. The

---

[73]Milton, *Paradise Lost*, 305-306.

Captain of the Serapis ordered the seamen to further weigh down the body so it could sink all the way. The sailors dully complied and the body vanished into the depths.[74]

In a similar scenario Asa Jenings, an American employee at Smyrna's YMCA, was on the deck of the USS Edsall when he heard a low cry from the water. As he looked over, he noticed a refugee struggling to stay afloat while U.S. sailors watched. Jennings chastised the men for their inaction and ordered them to lower a line, which they did. The refugee, a young freezing naked boy was hauled aboard. Immediately following the boy was his sister who the sailors also rescued. To facilitate her rescue, the ship's lights were turned off because Turkish snipers on shore were targeting the girl. Once aboard the barely revived girl was reunited with her brother.[75]

Eventually the international Commanders could not tolerate the atrocities and decided to take action to help the refugees despite the neutrality. Around midnight, on 13 September, British Admiral Brock capitulated to the repeated requests of Major Claflin Davis of the American Red Cross, and decided to aid the refugees. When the Allies sent boats to retrieve the victims, they became aware of the destruction's true extent. Charles Howes was one of the first to reach the quay with the mission of establishing a secure cordon so the refugees would not rush the boats. Howes witnessed horrendous scenes that were beyond his comprehension.[76]

The scene on the harbor as Howes describes it, was apocalyptic. The smell of burning flesh was in the air while dead bodies lined the streets. The collapsing houses and

[74]Ibid.

[75]Ibid., 373-375.

[76]Ibid., 342-343.

the wood crackling sounded like a salvo of guns. In the distance, he noticed a Turkish soldier throwing bodies of adults and children into the flames. Howes then witnessed a family with a father, a mother holding a baby and a young daughter making their way towards the rescue boat. Two shots killed the mother and the father. The mother immediately collapsed dropping the baby she was carrying. The nine-year old daughter picked the baby up and made her way to the boat.[77]

The rescue missions continued nonstop through the night and the following days while the Allies worked with the Kemalist to allow Greek ships to arrive and take the refugees. In the meantime, various humanitarian organizations rushed to provide aid. Dr. Esther Lovejoy was the Chairman of the Executive Board of the American Women's Hospitals and President of the Medical Women's International Association at the time. When the destruction occurred, she was immediately dispatched to Smyrna by the American Women's Hospitals. She was an eyewitness to the destruction and gave an interview in the *New York Times* describing the events. Below is her interview with the *New York Times* reporter:

> I was the first American Red Cross woman in France, she said, but what I saw there during the Great War seems a love feast beside the horrors of Smyrna. When I arrived at Smyrna there were massed on the quays 250,000 people . . . wretched, suffering and screaming . . . with women beaten and with their clothes torn off them, families separated and everybody robbed. Knowing their lives depended on escape before Sept.30, the crowds remained packed along the water front . . . so massed that there was no room to lie down. The sanitary conditions were unspeakable. Three-quarters of the crowd were women and children, and never have I seen so many women carry children. It seemed that every other woman was an expectant mother. The flight and the conditions brought on many premature births, and on the quay with scarcely room to lie down and without aid most of the children were born. In the five days I was there more than 200 such confinements occurred. Even more heartrending were the cries of children who

---

[77]Ibid.

had lost their mothers or mothers who had lost their children. They were herded along through the great guarded enclosure, and there was no turning back for lost ones. Mothers in the strength of madness climbed the steel fences fifteen feet high and in the face of blows from the butts of guns sought the children, who ran about screaming like animals.[78]

While waiting for the Greek ships to arrive, refugees' relied on their own wits to survive and that was certainly the case for Aristotle Onassis. His father had been imprisoned and awaiting deportation to central Anatolia, which meant certain death. His favorite uncle had been hanged while his other two uncles had been sent to the interior. Deportation meant a forced march where the elements or guards killed prisoners along the way. In one case over 5,000 prisoners left Smyrna, yet less than 500 reached Magnesia, only 30 miles away. Every few miles the guards executed groups of men. Aristotle knew that would be the fate of his father so he used bribes to secure his father's freedom and transportation on one of the warships. The Onassis family's deep pockets made their escape easy, which was not the case for the other victims who had to wait on the Greek ships.[79]

Eventually all refugees were evacuated after several days with the help of Allied and Greek ships. Estimates of the total human deaths and suffering vary greatly from source to source. Some estimates claim 120,000 victims, including women and children, 200,000 women molested, and hundreds of thousands evacuated. Smyrna, once an epicenter of western civilization, was now reduced to "a vast sepulcher of ashes."[80]

---

[78]"Woman Pictures Smyrna Horrors," *The New York Times*, 8 October 1922; Patterson, "Arlington National Cemetery."

[79]Milton, *Paradise Lost*, 361-364.

[80]"Smyrna's Ravagers Fired on Americans," *The New York Times,* 18 September 1922.

Ironically, the allied ships provided their greatest support to the Greco-Turkish cause, not by the actions they took, but by the stories they told. The international flotilla witnessing the destruction served to propagate the victims' stories around the world. The Smyrna holocaust was a culminating point of centuries of enmity galvanized by foreign meddling and a three-year war. Both nations suffered greatly and committed egregious acts during the three-year conflict.

Eventually the two nations involved agreed on a peaceful population exchange to prevent more such events or other incidental pogroms from occurring. The international community, which traditionally did not condone uprooting people from their hereditary homes, in this situation, agreed. The magnitude of the atrocities was so great that allowed no room or time for reconciliation. Perhaps the greatest supporters of separating the two nations were the individuals that lived through the disaster and were forever altered by the experience. Consul Horton would later write, "One of the keenest impressions which I brought away with me from Smyrna was a feeling of shame that I belonged to the human race."[81]

---

[81]Horton, *The Blight of Asia*, Chapter 10.

Photo Removed Due to Copyright Restrictions

Figure 3.   Smyrna: 1922

Source: Giles Milton, *Paradise Lost: Smyrna 1922: The Destruction of a Christian City in the Islamic World* (New York: Basic Books, 2008).

Photo Removed Due to Copyright Restrictions

Figure 4.   Atatürk Monument

Source: Historical sites and Monuments in Izmir, http://www.about-turkey.com/
tourism/monument1.htm (accessed 8 May 2012).
In the center of Cumhuriyet Meydani or Republic Square (in Izmir), is the Atatürk
Monument, an impressive statue of Atatürk sitting on horse and facing the sea. Erected in
1933, the monument commemorates the liberation of the city by Turkish forces.

CHAPTER 5

POPULATION EXCHANGE: PREVENTING

GENOCIDE AND MASS ATROCITIES

> Birth in one place,
> Growing old in another place.
> And feeling a stranger in two places.
>
> — Ayse Lahur Kirtunc, *Twice a Stranger*

Aaron, Abraham, Adam . . . books are filled with baby names neatly categorized to simplify choice. Selection of a child's name is done in a whimsical manner based more on trend rather than ancestry. This was not always the case in our culture and it certainly was not true for the Greeks in Asia Minor. Ethnic identity and religion were inescapably linked to every aspect of daily life. Beyond religious ceremonies, the Karamanlilar and the Rumlar held onto their ethnicity by their surnames and the names they chose for their children. Greek last names are mostly patronymic, but might also contain a suffix that indicates geographic origin. For example, Cretan last names end in "akis," such as Georgakis. Asia Minor Greeks followed a similar naming convention except their surname suffix was either "oglou," Turkish meaning son, or "ides" for males and "idou" for females. Last names, however, were not widely used early in the twentieth century.[82] As surnames became a necessity in the world, many individuals like Gabriel Isaakides remember how and when they were given a last name.

Gabriel, a Karamanli Greek, lived in the village of Uluağaç in central Turkey. One day in elementary school, his teacher was assigning surnames to the students. When

---

[82]Lexicon of Greek Personal Names, "The Transition to Modern Greek Names," http://www.lgpn.ox.ac.uk/names/modern.html (accessed 30 April 2012).

it was his turn, the teacher asked Gabriel for his grandfather's name. He answered Papa Isaac and the teacher responded with the surnames Papadopoulos and Isaakides. Out of respect to Orthodox priests, called "Papas", many took the last name Papadopoulos, meaning son of a priest. Isaakides eventually stuck with him until he was deracinated from this village and brought to his new country. It was not unusual for the school to shoulder the responsibility of such personal matters. For most Greeks the school and the church played prominent roles in everyday life.

Growing up in the village, Gabriel attended school six days a week. The curriculum included the usual subjects such as literature, history, and math as well as French. Sundays were observed for church services, which brought the entire community together. For the most part his life remained uneventful until around the age of ten. It was sometime after his tenth birthday that Gabriel's pregnant mother decided to venture to Constantinople and fetch her husband. Gabriel's father had gone to the big city to avoid being drafted into the infamous Turkish labor battalions, but rumors were circulating that he had a new love and was not returning. En route to Constantinople, his mother died possibly due to internal hemorrhaging. His father never returned. Five years later the now orphaned Gabriel also lost his country. A compulsory population exchange uprooted him and 1.2 million other Greeks living in Turkey as part of a controversial peace treaty.[83]

Following the Greco-Turkish war, peace between the two nations was negotiated at the Lausanne Conference. The Conference was held in Switzerland for 11 weeks, from 11 November 1922 to 24 July 1923. The main purpose of the conference was to replace

---

[83] Anastasia Isaakidou, daughter of Gabriel Isaakidou, interview by Jason Faulkenberry, 30 April 2012.

the Treaty of Sèvres, which was not recognized by Mustafa Kemal's new Turkish government. The main concerns debated were the Turkish territory in Europe and the Dardanelle Straits.[84] The key representatives at the conference included İsmet İnönü from Turkey, Lord Curzon who was the British Foreign Secretary, and Eleftherios Venizelos from Greece. At the time, Venizelos was not Prime Minister of Greece, but he was sent to negotiate the terms of the treaty because of his political acumen and his experience dealing with the nations involved.

As the Conference began the Turkish delegation made a surprising announcement. During one of the exchanges İsmet Pasha, the Turkish representative admitted to the banishment of nearly a million Orthodox Christians from Anatolia, and he declared the Turkish government would allow two weeks for the exodus. In response to his statement, the great powers heeded the warning and started developing evacuations plans. According to news reports of the time, the statesmen were worried the Christian minorities would have the same fate as the Armenians. A visit to Asia Minor by Fridtjof Nansen of the League of Nations further increased the urgency to remove Greeks from the region.[85]

Fridtjof Nansen was a Norwegian explorer and scientist who used his popularity for humanitarian purposes. In 1921, he was appointed as the League of Nation's High Commissioner for Refugees. Nansen was sent to Asia Minor to assess the situation and presented his report at the Lausanne conference. He recommended that all Greeks under

---

[84]"Allies in Agreement on Lausanne Demands," *The New York Times,* 17 November 1922.

[85]Edwin L.James, "Turks Proclaim Banishment Edict to 1,000,000 Greeks," *The New York Times*, 2 December 1922.

Turkish sovereignty be removed quickly to rescue them from starvation or death by other

means. The High Commissioner's statement made it obvious that the evacuation of

Greeks from Turkish territory expanded beyond the simple prisoner of war exchange.[86]

Responding to his remarks, İsmet Pasha stated that the Turks were willing to discuss all

the Greeks leaving Turkey. Consequently, İsmet's remarks spurred the following events

according to the *New York Times*:

> Lord Curzon declared that he felt that many thousands of lives were at stake and
> said that quick action must be taken. He said that the Turks had decreed that all
> Greeks in Anatolia must get out by the last day of November and added that they
> had extended the date to 15 Dec. Immediate steps, Lord Curzon said, must be
> taken to remove the Greeks by that date.[87]

İsmet concurred with Curzon's arguments and stated that the Greeks in

Constantinople should also depart. Curzon then reminded the Turkish representative of

the Turks living in Greece. Curzon warned that Muslims in Greece could suffer

retaliation if Greek minorities in Turkey were harmed. İsmet simply replied that it might

be a good idea to trade populations. Finally, the discussion concluded with the

appointment of a subcommittee to consider means for removing the Greeks from Turkish

lands.[88] Eleven days later on 12 December 1922, returning to the subject, Lord Curzon

stated that Muslims in Western Thrace could stay in Greece if Turkey allowed the Greeks

---

[86]Ibid.

[87]Ibid.

[88]Ibid.

to remain in Constantinople. Turkey finally ceded and allowed the exclusion of the Greeks in Constantinople from the proposed population exchange.[89]

The exclusion of Constantinople was important because it was the location of the Greek Orthodox Patriarchate and would cause public uproar in the Christian world. Retaining the patriarchate in Constantinople was a solution the American delegation advocated. Lord Curzon agreed with the U.S. and further stated the whole world would arise if the expulsion took place.[90] Later during the Peace Treaty of 24 July 1923, the island of Imvros and Tenedos' Orthodox Christians were also excluded. The two islands are positioned near the Dardanelles straits and strategically important to the Allies.[91] With these stipulations in place, a population exchange started to materialize. According to news reports, Allied diplomats admitted to the plan's inhumanity but defended the propositions stating it was the only way of preventing a worse fate for the Greeks in Turkey.[92]

Lord Curzon expressed the same sentiment as the other diplomats as he stated in a poignant speech delivered at the conference. A newspaper at the time reported the following about Curzon's speech:

> In a speech at today's session Lord Curzon expressed the deepest regret at the necessity of deciding on an exchange of populations, but declared that a week's discussion showed that no other decision was possible. Admitting that he detested

---

[89]Edwin L. James, "American Envoy Asks Guarantees for Minorities," *The New York Times*, 13 December 1922.

[90]Edwin L. James, "Million Must Quit Homes in Near East Lausanne Decrees," *The New York Times*, 11 January 1923.

[91]Hirschon, *Crossing the Aegean*, 8.

[92]James, "Million Must Quit Homes in Near East Lausanne Decrees."

the solution and deplored it, he said he thought there was nothing else to do. What he meant was that there was no way of preventing Turkey from ousting the Greeks unless the Allies were prepared to fight, and , like the Americans, the English are not ready to fight the Turks for humanitarian ends.[93]

Possibly the best insight on the reason behind the population exchange came from another newspaper article published the day after the convention was signed. It indicated Turkey was headed towards a Greek Genocide articulated in the following:

> But it should be said in extenuation of the surrender at Lausanne that the allied diplomats were confronted with three facts: Before the World War there were three millions of Greeks in Turkish territory; a million of them were killed or dispersed in 1915; a million and a half of them, since 1915, have been killed or dispersed (dispersal being the more merciless method of driving them to arid plateaus where they died lingeringly from starvation), and the events at Smyrna were still fresh before the minds of the delegates. What assurances could there be against further massacres and forcible deportations if these helpless and peaceable folk were left at the mercy of the Turk?[94]

On 30 January 1923, the population exchange mandated by the Convention Concerning the Exchange of Greek and Turkish Populations and Protocol was signed at Lausanne, Switzerland. The convention was comprised of 19 Articles that provided general instructions on matters such as milestones, deadlines, who was included and who was exempt. In addition, the convention set up a Mixed Commission to supervise the exchange and oversee property liquidation, handling, and compensation. The exchange involved Turkish nationals of Greek Orthodox faith and Muslim Greek nationals. Religion was the sole defining criterion of identity, a relic of the Ottoman times. Another unique Convention element was the inclusion of a clause that ensured those who had previously fled would not be allowed to return. Accordingly, the convention stated,

---

[93]Ibid.

[94]Bent, "Uprooting of Greeks in Turkey A Modern Exodus of Outcasts."

"These persons shall not return to live in Turkey or Greece without the authorization of the Turkish Government or the Greek Government respectively."[95]

Exemptions to the exchange were addressed in the Convention's Article 2. The two main groups that were excluded were the Greeks of Constantinople and the Turks of Western Thrace. In a glance it might seem illogical to move certain people yet exclude others but the strategic objectives and public opinion discussed before ensured certain minorities remained outside of the exchange. The following Article 3 explicitly guaranteed that all refugees who had already left their homes, regardless of reason, were included in the exchange. The subsequent articles directed the actual exchange by first setting an order of precedence. Providing some insight to the concerns of the time, the first installment of Greeks exchanged, according to Article 4, were all able-bodied men detained by Turkey. This provision further demonstrated that the Allied statesmen were worried of the immediate safety of those men.[96]

In extensive detail, the remaining 15 Articles describe all aspects of the exchange to include prohibition of governmental obstacles, loss and receipt of nationality, and allotted timetables for implementation actions. The Mixed Commission was specifically directed to accomplish several functions to facilitate a successful emigration. Emphasis was further placed on the handling of property including shipping, liquidating and compensating refugees. Article 8, for instance, states the populations would be free to take with them "their movable property of every kind" and they will not have to pay any

---

[95]Lausanne Peace Treaty VI (Convention concerning the Exchange of Greek and Turkish Populations and Protocol, signed at Lausanne 30 January 1923), 7.

[96]Ibid., 2.

taxes. If the emigrants are not able to remove their property local authorities will create an inventory and valuation of the items left behind. Finally, the authorities will make four copies of the inventory holding one for them, providing a copy to the government of the emigrant, one to the individual and a copy will be sent to the Mixed Commission.[97] At first glance the convention with the explicit directions seemed likely to succeed yet the execution proved otherwise.

The circumstances in Greece and Turkey were so different at the time resulting in an asymmetric experience for the two nations. According to professor of social anthropology, Renee Hirschon the imbalance was due to the different historical and political significance the exchange had on the two countries and on the scale of the populations involved. Dr. Hirschon's *Crossing the Aegean*, states the event was a culminating point for the victorious Turks. Mustafa Kemal Atatürk salvaged the remnants of the Ottoman Empire, expelled all foreigners and established a new republic. In contrast, Greece called the event the Asia Minor Catastrophe that ended with the decisive Greek defeat and the population exchange. The calamitous events of the Greco-Turkish War had significant implications for Greek politicians since anyone associated with the catastrophe fell from the public's graces. In Greece, political change over and instability exacerbated the ongoing turmoil following the war.[98]

The disparity in the populations also resulted in an asymmetric experience for the two nations. Greece's population at the time of the exchange totaled about 4.5 million. The influx of 1.2 million refugees increased the population by a quarter in just two years.

---

[97]Ibid.

[98]Hirschon, *Crossing the Aegean*, 13-15.

That is the equivalent of the U.S. today growing by 78,358,659 in two years. Such a tremendous increase would have a significant impact on any nation, but it would be even greater for a bankrupt nation, recovering from a war. On the other hand, the population expelled to Turkey numbered only 355,635. Turkey's population at the time was estimated at 13.5 million, which meant the influx constituted less than four percent of the total population. Such a small increase over two years barely affected the nation's economy. In contrast, the Christian population's departure hurt Turkey the most.[99]

With the Christian exodus, Turkey lost most of its entrepreneurial class. Trade, finance, and industry were mostly accomplished by Greeks. The massive departure of these specialties along with the destruction of Smyrna tremendously affected the regional economy as an international trading link was disrupted. The influx of Muslims from Greece was largely small-scale farmers who could not fill the gap, but could become quickly self-sufficient. In contrast, Greece gained new skills and industries from the Anatolians. As industries benefited by the influx of skilled workers, the nation languished attempting to support its new found citizens. Greece felt a great economic burden while resettling the refugees. In the 1930s, the refugee settlement contributed to the country's bankruptcy and continuing economic crises.[100]

The exchange's cultural impact was also unequal for the two nations. Greece witnessed a revival of Byzantine art and music. The Orthodox Church experienced a rebirth while the refugee experience spawned a new urban popular music genre. A flurry of traditional music and dance was further influenced by the Asia Minor Greeks. A

---

[99]Ibid.

[100]Ibid., 16-17.

unique style of literature that yearned for the lost homeland emerged. The Anatolians also greatly influenced Greek cuisine, which also became associated with their identity. In contrast, the cultural effects on Turkey were insignificant. This again was mostly due to the relative small number of individuals that were exchanged.[101]

In both nations, the newly arriving populace was initially welcomed with celebrations and sympathy, but the relations between the locals and the emigrants quickly soured. The political turmoil, the economic downturn and the issues associated with accommodating the influx of people flared animosity. Several pejorative terms were used for the Asia Minor Greeks by mainland Greeks to include Turkish seeds (tourkospori), orientals (anatolites) and baptized in yogurt (yiaourtovaptismeni). The last term originates from the pervasive use of yogurt in Greek emigrant cuisine. The Turks who came from Greece did not fare much better as they were often called half infidel (yari gavur). Beyond pejorative names and their unique surnames, the newly arrived emigrants were also easily discerned by their houses and communities in which they resided.[102]

Once more, the housing and settlement experience was unequal for the two nations. Since the Muslims of Greece displaced nearly four-times as many Asia Minor Greeks, numerous houses were available to them. Even today, entire villages like Kayaköy, remain uninhabited ghost towns. Greece on the other hand, could not keep up with the resettlement rate so several refugees took matters into their own hands. To mitigate the resettlement rate Greece and the League of Nations established the Refugee Settlement Commission. The Refugee Settlement Commission was an autonomous

---

[101]Ibid., 18-19.

[102]Clark, *Twice a Stranger*, 32.

organization that channeled and controlled aid for refugee resettlement. Yet even the Refugee Settlement Commission and the abandonment of Muslim properties were insufficient. As the newly vacated Muslim residents were about a fourth of the required number, refugees built ad hoc houses and communities. The result was a chaotic urban space that even today encumbers the landscape of Greece.[103]

The Greeks that were exempt from the population exchange did not fare much better than those expelled as over time they were subjected to governmental punitive measures. In 1932, the Turkish parliament passed a law that barred Greek citizens in Turkey from 30 key professions and trades. Then in 1942, a Wealth Tax was imposed almost exclusively on Greeks and Jews attempting to curtail their economic potential in Turkey. Anti-Greek sentiment came to a climax in September 1955 with government sponsored Istanbul pogroms. The Turkish government spread fabricated stories that Atatürk's house in Thessalonica (city in Northern Greece) was attacked by rioting Greeks. The lie incited attacks against Greek businesses and civilians. Because of these and other anti-Greek actions, by 1967 almost the entire Istanbul Greek community was expelled from Turkey. Thus, even the groups that were spared from the population exchange eventually suffered the same, albeit protracted, consequences.[104]

---

[103]Vassilis Colonas, "Housing and the Architectural Expression of Asia Minor Greeks Before and After 1923," in *Crossing the Aegean An Appraisal of the 1923 Compusory Population Exchange Between Greece and Turkey*, ed. Renee Hirschon (New York: Oxford, 2008), 168.

[104]Alexandris, "Religion or Ethinicity," 119.

CHAPTER 6

GENOCIDE AND MASS ATROCITIES PREVENTED

> I have issued the command . . . and I'll have anybody who utters but one word of criticism executed by firing squad . . . that our war aim does not consist of reaching certain lines, but in the physical destruction of the enemy. Accordingly, I have placed my death-head formations in readiness . . . for the present only in the East . . . with orders to them to send to death mercilessly and without compassion, men, women, and children of Polish derivation and language. Only thus shall we gain the living space (Lebensraum) which we need. Who, after all, speaks today of the annihilation of the Armenians?[105]

In early June 1915, nineteen-year-old Armenian Soghomon Tehlirian and his family were rounded up by Turkish forces with 20,000 other Armenians in his hometown of Erzinga. Before the deportation began, all valuables besides what could be carried were forcefully surrendered to Turkish authorities for safekeeping. Once the column marched for several hours, the gendarmes searched and stole from the deportees what little they had not turned in. In an instant, total havoc broke loose. Shots rang out, several soldiers dragged away and raped Tehlirian's sister while another split his brother's head with an axe. Just as he noticed his mother's body on the ground, he was suddenly struck on the head and fell unconscious. When he awoke, it was dark and something heavy was on his chest. He struggle to get up only to notice his brother's corpse was weighing him

---

[105]Adolf Hitler, Obersalzberg, 22 August 1939, speech delivered by Hitler to the Supreme Commanders and Commanding Generals; as stated by Former Bureau Chief of the Associated Press in Berlin, Louis Lochner, in his book *What About Germany*? (New York: Dodd, Mead, and Company, 1942), 2. This particular language does not appear in any of the other primary source accounts of Hitler's speech.

down. As he looked around, he realized with horror that he was the sole survivor of the entire caravan. His was not the only such story.[106]

In the years following the Armenian Genocide, thousands of survivors and other witnesses came forward with equally horrific stories. Unfortunately, Hitler's assumption in his 1939 speech to the Supreme Commanders and Commanding Generals was correct. Few today recall or are aware of the Armenian annihilation, the twentieth century's first genocide.[107] Yet the individuals directly affected and witnessing those events will never forget. Such was the case with the Asia Minor Greeks who were familiar and apprehensive of the Armenian fate. The two Christian minorities had coexisted and, at times, commiserated under Ottoman rule. In fact, along with the Armenians, 50 percent of the Pontian population was also exterminated. Pontians were a small group of Greeks living around the coastal area of the Black Sea.[108]

By all accounts, the Greeks were rightfully fearful. Unbeknownst to them, all the indicators for a potential genocide were present at the time. Genocide scholars claim a previous act of genocide alone is one the best predictors of a future occurrence.[109] Other

---

[106]Edward Alexander, *A Crime of Vengeance: An Armenian Struggel for Justice* (New York: The Free Prees, 1991), 69-70.

[107]Ronald Levitsky, *The Pontian Greek Genocide: A Teaching Unit* (Chicago: Pontian Society of Chicago, 2006), 6.

[108]Greek-Genocide.org, "Greek Genocide 1914-23," http://www.greek-genocide.org/pontus.html (accessed 18 April 2012).

[109]Harold M. Schulweis, "Human Rights in Crises: A Summary for Jewish World Watch," JewishWorldWatch.org, 2 June 2008, http://www.jewishworldwatch.org/wp-content/uploads/2010/06/wc_Jun2008.pdf (accessed 18 April 2012).

scholars claim the denial of genocide is the best hint of a future act.[110] Either way, both situations were true in this case providing more credibility to an ensuing genocide. Even more alarming was the presence of other genocide indicators. Genocide scholar Dr. Gregory H. Stanton asserts there are eight "predictable but not inexorable" stages to genocide.[111] These eight stages were all present. Thus, the existence and denial of the Armenian-Pontian Genocide, the atrocities at Smyrna, along with other indicators pointed to a coming genocide. Luckily, the population exchange halted the process. In order to support this assertion, however, the definition of genocide must first be addressed.

Definition of Genocide

The second chapter in Samantha Power's seminal book, *A Problem from Hell* is titled "A Crime without a Name." It is hard to believe that until 1943, when Raphael Lemkin coined the term, the crime of genocide was nameless. Ironically, it was the incidents following the Armenian annihilation that spurred him to come up with the word. Raphael Lemkin was studying linguistics at the University of Lvov when he first read a newspaper article on the assassination of Talaat Pasha. Talaat, the Armenian Genocide's main perpetrator, was assassinated in the streets of Berlin by a student named Soghomon Tehlirian.[112] Tehlirian shouted, "This is to avenge the death of my family!" as he shot Talaat in the head. Lemkin was perplexed that Tehlirian was charged with murder yet Talaat was not. Lemkin's professor explained there was no law under which Talaat

---

[110]The Armenian Genocide, "Recognition," http://www.mtholyoke.edu/ ~kotik22a/classweb/armenian_genocide/why_matters.html (accessed 18 April 2012).

[111]Stanton, *The Eight Stages of Genocide*.

[112]"Talaat Pasha Slain in Berlin Suburb," *The New York Times*, 16 March 1921.

could be charged. This galvanized the young Jewish Pole to develop a term and later legislation, unique to this crime.[113]

The final definition came in Lemkin's 1943 book titled *Axis Rule in Occupied Europe*. He combined two terms, the Greek word *genos*, for race or people, with the suffix cide, meaning to kill. The resulting was the compound word we use today. In his book, Lemkin defined genocide as follows:

> Generally speaking, genocide does not necessarily mean the immediate destruction of a nation, except when accomplished by mass killings of all members of a nation. It is intended rather to signify a coordinated plan of different actions aiming at the destruction of essential foundations of the life of national groups, with the aim of annihilating the groups themselves. The objectives of such a plan would be the disintegration of the political and social institutions, of culture, language, national feelings, religion, and the economic existence of national groups, and the destruction of the personal security, liberty, health, dignity, and even the lives of the individuals belonging to such groups.[114]

Scholars studying the subject tried to fine tune the definition over the years, however, the law binding verbiage is the United Nations Definition in Article 2 and adopted by Resolution 260 (III) A of the United Nations General Assembly on 9 December 1948. According to the United Nations, genocide is defined as:

> Article II: In the present Convention, genocide means any of the following acts committed with intent to destroy, in whole or in part, a national, ethnical, racial or religious group, as such: (a) Killing members of the group; (b) Causing serious bodily or mental harm to members of the group; (c) Deliberately inflicting on the group conditions of life calculated to bring about its physical destruction in whole or in part; (d) Imposing measures intended to prevent births within the group; (e) Forcibly transferring children of the group to another group.

---

[113]Power, *A Problem from Hell*, 1-29.

[114]Gregory H. Stanton, "What is Genocide?" *Genocide Watch*, http://www.genocidewatch.org/genocide/whatisit.html (accessed 18 April 2012).

Furthermore, according to Article III, the following acts shall be punishable: (a) Genocide; (b) Conspiracy to commit genocide; (c) Direct and public incitement to commit genocide; (d) Attempt to commit genocide; (e) Complicity in genocide.[115]

In the definition of genocide, the phrase "in whole or in part" is not coincidental, as perpetrators need not intend to destroy the entire group. Furthermore even the partial destruction of groups like the intelligentsia or members residing in one region, is also genocide. Paradoxically under this definition an individual may be criminal guilty of genocide even if he killed only one person. If that individual knew he was participating in a larger plan to destroy a group, then that is considered genocide. Lastly, the law is designed to protect national, ethnic, racial or religious groups.[116] This definition then must be considered when evaluating the circumstance of the Greco-Turkish conflict.

The Armenian and Pontian Annihilation

The Christian minorities' destiny fluctuated along with the political situation in the Ottoman Empire. During times of tranquility and peace, the Greeks were the most significant beneficiaries of all the Christian minorities. This was due to certain ancestral advantages. The Seljuk Turks defeated and thus adopted lands previously under the Byzantine Empire. The Eastern Empire was an offshoot of the Roman Empire, centered on the capital of Byzantium later known as Constantinople. Unlike the Roman Empire, it was Christian and by all accounts Greek. The *lingua franca* and the cultural orientation were both Greek. The Bible, the centerpiece of Byzantine and Christian life, was also

---

[115]William A. Schabas, "Convention on the Prevention and Punishment of the Crime of Genocide," United Nations Audiovisual Library of International Law, Resolution 260 (III) A of the U.N. General Assembly, 9 December 1948, entered into force, 12 January 1951.

[116]Stanton, "What is Genocide?"

64

written in Greek. Due to this hereditary advantage, the Greeks were utilized extensively in the Ottoman Empire in various prestigious positions.[117]

One such group that eventually gained political power in the Ottoman court was the Phanariotes or the Phanariote Greeks. This prominent group name came from the Phanar quarter of Constantinople near the Ecumenical Patriarchate (akin to Greek Orthodox Pope). Phanariotes were wealthy and well-educated merchants that held powerful political and administrative posts in the Ottoman Empire. Due to their high level of education, the Phanariotes comprised the majority of the Sultan's and other officials' *dragomans* or interpreters and foreign liaison officers. Eventually the Phanariotes played a prominent role in Greece's independence from the Empire and thus the group fell from power and the Sultan's graces.[118]

The elite Janissaries have a comparable story and suffered a similar fate as the Phanariotes. Janissaries (or *Yeni Ceri* meaning New Army) were an elite Ottoman infantry unit. They comprised the Sultan's personal bodyguards and his most prized soldiers. The unit was the best-trained, educated and equipped Ottoman force. They wore a standardized unique uniform exclusively made by the Sephardic Jewish tailors in Thessaloniki. Recruitment for the unit was controversial. Young Balkan Christian boys were collected through the blood-tax of *devshirme* (child gathering). Some recruits were forcefully taken while others were volunteered by their families since the Janissaries could rise to powerful positions. The children were converted to Islam before beginning

---

[117]Dr. Vook, *The Byzantine Empire 101: The Textvook* (Vook, 2011).

[118]Suraiya Faroqhi, *Subjects of the Sultan* (New York: I. B.Tauris and Co. Ltd., 2007), 48.

official military training. This elite unit grew to wield great political power and attempted to extort more money and privileges from the Sultan. Eventually the Janissaries were disbanded, but their constant struggles with the Sultan and other officials greatly contributed to the Ottoman Empire's deterioration.[119]

As the Empire began to disintegrate and lose major battles, the situation worsened for both the Greeks and the Armenians. In the late 1800s, the Ottoman Empire began a steady decline and was often referred to as the "Sick Man of Europe." In 1908, the Young Turks revolted against Sultan Abdul-al-Hamid II and gained control of the government. Initially the movement appeared hospitable to all minorities and this was a welcome reprieve for all. After the Ottoman defeat in the Balkan Wars of 1912 and 1913, the attitude soon changed. A Young Turks nationalist group called the Committee of Union and Progress took control of the government. The Committee of Union Progress's goals were geared in strengthening the Empire economically and militaristically. In order to achieve those goals the new government focused on Turkification which entailed elimination of ethnic Christian minorities.[120]

By 1914 a Young Turks fraction led by Enver Pasha and Talaat Bey controlled the government and initiated an all out attack on Christians. Under the slogan "Turkey for the Turks," property was confiscated while the owners were either indiscriminately slaughtered or deported to the interior. As is the modus operandi in numerous genocides, the prominent figures in each town were first targeted for persecution. This included town

---

[119]David Nicolle, *Armies of the Ottoman Turks 1300-1774* (London: Osprey, 1983), 9-11.

[120]Halo, *Not Even my Name*, 117-119.

clergymen, teachers, businessmen and all of the community's intelligentsia. U.S. consul general at Smyrna George Horton stated in his diary dated 11 December 1910 that the aggressors had initiated a "series of assassinations of chiefs of communities, in broad day, in the streets." At the same time, surprisingly, the Greeks of Asia Minor (specifically Smyrna) were not molested.[121]

The U.S. Consul George Horton was in charge of Entente interests in Asia Minor and was in contact with Rehmi Bey, a war governor-general. Bey explained to Horton the Greek subjects in Asia Minor were not disturbed because King Constantine was an ally of Turkey, preventing Greece from going into war. Interestingly, the *Rayas* or Greek Ottoman subjects of the Port were extensively maltreated. Ottoman Greek businesses were boycotted and anti-Christian propaganda posters and articles started circulating in the press. According to Horton, cheap lithographs depicted Greeks cutting up Turkish babies and ripping open pregnant Muslim women. These baseless scenes were hung in mosques and schools and had immediate results. Sporadic assassinations and pogroms erupted throughout Asia Minor. The situation only worsened with the First World War.[122] According to Ottoman law, non-Muslim men were prohibited from carrying arms and, therefore, during wartime were sent to the interior and assigned to work battalions. The conditions at the work battalion were atrocious. A large number perished from exposure to the elements, hunger, disease or exhaustion. This process effectively eliminated young males of military age and ensured the minorities could not aid enemy forces, mainly the Russians in the case of the Armenians or the Allies for the Greeks. Eventually with war

---

[121]Ibid.

[122]Horton, *The Blight of Asia*, 326.

as a backdrop the Young Turks and later the Kemalist, continued and even increased a systemic elimination of Greeks and Armenians. This was the case with the Greeks of Pontus or Pontians.[123]

Pontus is ancient Greek for "sea" referring to the Black Sea and the surrounding coastal areas. In search for gold, the Greeks established colonies in the region around 1000 B.C. some 2,000 years before the migration of Turkic people to the region. Several wealthy cities were established among them Sinope, Samsun and Trebizond. The Pontus region is believed to be the site of several myths including the land of the Amazons where Prometheus was punished and the Golden Fleece sought by Jason and the Argonauts. Pontus was also the birthplace of Diogenes, one of the founders of Cynic philosophy, along with the famous geographer Strabo.[124]

Under Ottoman rule, the Pontians faired like other Christian minorities, as times of tranquility were separated by occasional pogroms and persecution. The major shift occurred with the outbreak of WWI in 1914. Using the vulnerability of the Black Sea coast to Russian attack as a pretext, the Turkish government started mass deportations of Pontic Greeks along with others to the interior of the country. Tens of thousands died as they were forcibly marched in the middle of winter as far south as the Syrian Desert. From 1914 to 1918, the deportations alone caused the death of over 100,000 Pontians. In addition, Turkish police and irregular forces, claiming to be searching for deserters, raided villages raping, stealing and murdering.[125]

---

[123]Levitsky, *The Pontian Greek Genocide.*

[124]Ibid., 12.

[125]Ibid., 16.

68

A second phase of attacks started on 19 May 1919 when Kemalist forces entered

Samsun. Topal Osman Pasha led government and irregular forces that indiscriminately

destroyed villages killing innocent men, women and children. From 1919 to 1922, nearly

150,000 additional Greeks were murdered. These incidents, most likely, were in

retaliation to for the Greek military occupation of Smyrna and the atrocities the soldiers

committed during their retreat. Furthermore, Turkey needed to secure ports on the Black

Sea to help establish trade with their new found ally, Russia. In the meantime,

international communities aware of the atrocities failed to intervene.[126]

Numerous reliable sources witnessed and reported the atrocities. Two such

sources were Forest Yowell and Mark Ward. Yowell was the Director of the Harpoot

Unit of the American relief organization called Near East Relief. Ward was the Medical

director of Near East Relief. They jointly sent a letter on 5 April 1922 to Jesse B. Jackson

who was serving as U.S. consul in Aleppo, Syria. Jackson forwarded this letter to the

U.S. Secretary of State in Washington on 6 April 1922 along with other related

documents. The information and the figures in the letter are from American eyewitness

sources that Forest Yowell and Mark Ward vouch for their accuracy. One paragraph

describes the intent and the circumstances associated with the deportations.

> Of the entire number of Greeks deported, about two thirds of them were women
> and children and the main causes of death were, starvation, exposure, typhus, and
> dysentery. The Turkish authorities were frank in their statements that it was the
> intention to have all the Greeks die and all of their actions . . . their failure to
> supply any food or clothing . . . their strong opposition to relief by the N. E. R. . . .
> their choice of route, weather, etc. . . . . concentrations in unhealthful places, and
> last of all their deliberate choice of destination BITLIS, a place almost totally
> destroyed, with no industry and located far up in the mountains, seem to fully bear

---

[126]Ibid., 18.

69

this statement out. All along the route of the deportees, Moslems visit the various groups and take of the women and girls whomever they want for immoral purposes.[127]

The final casualty numbers of the Pontic Greek extermination vary greatly although a conservative estimate is about 250,000. Even though that number seems relatively low when compared to the Armenian Genocide, the Turks effectively exterminated approximately 50 percent of the Pontian Greeks. The world may not be aware of this statistic, but all the Greeks are. In fact, this knowledge made Greek Prime Minister Eleftherios Venizelos relatively uneasy especially on the eve of the Greco-Turkish War. Venizelos also used the protection of Greek minorities as a pretext to land troops in Smyrna. Further exacerbating his fears was the knowledge of the Armenian fate. The Pontic annihilation, not a unique occurrence, was executed simultaneously and in the same manner as the Armenian Genocide.[128]

The atrocities against the Armenians did not occur spontaneously as a single incident, but over an extended period. According to Taner Akcam, author of *A Shameful Act: The Armenian Genocide and the Question of Turkish Responsibility*, the genocide was a series of events orchestrated by the Ottomans-Turks against their Armenian subjects. Dr. Akcam asserts the Turkish persecution of Armenians was multi-faceted. First, under the pretext of tax collection, pursuit of military deserters, and pacification of rebellions, Ottomans routinely attacked Armenian villages. Second, centrally organized

---

[127]Mark H. Ward and Forrest D. Yowell, "Archival Document Project," *Greek-Genocide.org,* 5 April 1922, http://www.greek-genocide.org/documents.html (accessed 18 April 2012).

[128]Greek-Genocide.org, Greek Genocide 1914-23, http://www.greek-genocide.org/pontus.html (accessed 18 April 2012).

pogroms were organized in border villages by the Ottoman Special Organization units. Finally, deportations via forced marches, led to the death of many Armenians.[129]

The Armenian genocide can be separated into two periods prior and post to 1915. Although both, according to Akcam, were the product of the central Ottoman government, the massacres preceding 1915 were local in nature. In 1890, Sultan Abdul Hamid II created a paramilitary organization called the Hamidiye regiment, formed of Kurdish cavalry forces. The regiment's focus was to bind the Muslim population to the Sultan and cow Armenians into submission. Nevertheless, the outbreak of WWI allowed the Turks to take definitive actions against the Armenians without the constant pressure of outside powers. Therefore, following 1915, the Hamidiye regiment along with newly formed irregular militias comprised of Kurdish members and jailed convicts continued the pogroms of Armenian villages. Secondly, the Sultan declared the Armenians a suspect national group and placed them into labor groups where many lost their lives due to deprivation, exposure, and torture. Lastly, masses of Armenians where forcefully deported and either executed during the process or simply died of natural causes or from disease and starvation.[130]

It is unclear why Turkish animosity towards Armenians escalated to such levels but foreign pressure and meddling certainly exacerbated the situation. Before WWI, Russia desired an autonomous Armenia, which the Ottomans viewed as a ploy for territorial gains and the Ottoman Empire's eventual demise. In late December 1914 early January 1915, the Ottomans suffered an embarrassing defeat at the Battle of Sarıkamış by

---

[129]Akcam, *A Shameful Act*, 19-49, 111-148.

[130]Ibid.

the defending Russian army. Simultaneously, Turkish forces were aggressively engaged in a campaign in Gallipoli. Threatened on both fronts, the Turks believed the Armenians would aid the British landing at Iskenderun and further support Russian forces as they had in the past. The Armenians' past support to Russians greatly fomented Turkish animosity. Eventually Russia and Turkey became allies, yet Turkish hostility towards the Armenians persisted. Regardless of the means or motives, Turkish actions resulted in an estimated one to one and a half million Armenian casualties.

The significance of Smyrna

The crescendo of Greco-Turkish enmity was the destruction of Smyrna. The sheer brutality was an ominous indicator of an even greater potential calamity. Beyond the acts of violence, the city's destruction greatly injured the Greek and Turkish psyches. It is hard to imagine, but Smyrna at its time was regarded as a cosmopolitan city comparable to London, Paris or New York. The city had 23 newspapers printed in various languages, 391 factories and a bustling port.[131] Linking Asia to Europe, goods were exported around the world. The great mills of Nazli supplied flour to Turkey and the rest of Europe. The city was lauded as an example of tolerance where Jewish, Armenian, Levantine, Greek, and Turkish coexisted and thrived. As U.S. Consul Horton stated, "In no city in the world did East and West mingle physically in so spectacular a manner as at Smyrna, while spiritually they always maintained the characteristics of oil and water."[132]

---

[131]Dobkin, *Smyrna 1922 The Destruction of a City*, 107.

[132]Horton, *The Blight of Asia*, 949.

Smyrna and the surrounding region in Asia Minor was a spiritual epicenter for early Christians. Christianity's national importance to Greece is evident by prominent cross on the country's flag. As such, the lands in Turkey were deeply coveted culturally and spiritually. After all, the great Christian assemblies where held at nearby Nicea, Ephesus, and Chalcedon. The author of a large part of the New Testament, the apostle Paul came from Tarsus, and lived in neighboring Ephesus. Gregory the Theologian, one of the Three Holy Hierarchs and Doctor of the Church, also came from Nanzanius in Asia Minor. In addition, all seven major Churches of early Christianity were located around Smyrna in Asia Minor. Jesus Christ, in the New Testament, instructs John to write a letter to the seven churches that include Ephesus, Smyrna, Pergamum, Thyatira, Sardis, Philadelphia, and Laodicea.[133]

Ephesus, Smyrna, and the nearby cities were also tremendous cultural centers. Two of the seven wonders of the ancient world were in Asia Minor near Smyrna. The Temple of Artemis at Ephesus and the Mausoleum of Halicarnassus attracted and continue to attract scores of tourists. Scholars were also enticed by two prominent schools in Smyrna, the Homerion and the Evangelical School for Boys. The latter was renowned for its library that contained valuable, books, manuscripts, and inscriptions, which have never been replaced since the city's destruction. The Homerion, on the other hand, was named from Homer, the city's most notable residents. Consul Horton wrote the following about the Ionian region:

> From Ionia, the mother civilization spread to old Greece, to Sicily, to Italy and along the shores of the Black Sea, and finally to Europe and America! It is more than probable that Homer was a Smyrniote, or an inhabitant of Asia Minor, and

---

[133]Revelations 1:11.

for countless years his writings were a sort of Bible or sacred book, molding the character of millions. Perhaps the earliest conception of monogamy, certainly the most beautiful, comes from Homer's poems. Our conception of the family is Greek; we get it from the Odyssey, very probably written in Smyrna, thousands of years ago.[134]

The Turks coveted the city and the region for many of the same reasons as the Greeks. The city was a source of wealth and pride. As mentioned, it was often celebrated as an example of Ottoman tolerance where minorities peacefully coexisted. Most importantly, the city had several hegemons in its history but the last several hundred years it was ruled successfully by Ottomans. During Turkey's war of independence, Greek occupation of Smyrna possibly spurred the nation's spirit unlike anything before. When the Pasha signed the armistice and the treaties, he anticipated the possibility of British troops landing on Turkish soil. Occupation by a nation that was subjugated by Ottomans for several centuries was extremely insulting. George Horton wrote the Turkish sentiment to Greeks landing in Smyrna was comparable to if Mobile, Alabama "were given over to a mandate of negro troops."[135] Unfortunately, the events that followed demonstrated the veracity of Horton's statement.

Eight Stages of Genocide

Professor Gregory H. Stanton is the founder of Genocide Watch and author of *The 8 Stages of Genocide*. From 1992 to 1999, Dr. Stanton served in the State Department where he drafted United Nations Security Council resolutions. According to Stanton, genocide is a non-linear process that develops in eight stages. The stages operate

---

[134]Horton, *The Blight of Asia*, 883.

[135]Ibid., 672.

throughout the process and include classification, symbolization, dehumanization, organization, polarization, preparation, extermination and lastly denial. The author asserts the stages are predictable, but not inexorable and preventive measures can stop the process at each stage.[136] In response to the collapsing empire and the ensuing paranoia along with retaliation for Greek atrocities, the Turks were headed towards genocide of the Greek minority.

Classification

The Ottoman Empire from early in its history classified its subjects and communities for administrative and taxation reasons. Since it was a theocracy, individuals under the Ottoman rule were subjects not citizens. Islam was the state religion, other monotheistic faiths, known as "people of the book" were recognized and enjoyed relative autonomy. Non-Muslim under Sharia law, were afforded the *dhimmi* status. Accordingly, the *dhimmi* received protection in return for taxation called *jizya*. Life, property and freedom of religion were all guaranteed but the subjects were obliged to display subservience and loyalty to the Muslim order. Therefore, when the *dhimmi* did not uphold their responsibility, they forfeited their protection rights. By all accounts, the Ottoman Empire tolerated new religions but by no means held them as equals to Islam.[137]

The *dhimmi* were further classified into religious groups and organizations called millets. Education, adjudication, rituals, marriages, inheritance were administered by the autonomous millet system. The millet source of authority came from a Sultanic Letter of

---

[136]Stanton, *The Eight Stages of Genocide*.

[137]Akcam, *A Shameful Act*, 19-49.

Permission. Traditionally, a high-ranking clergyman was chosen as community leader and responsible to the sultan. For Ottomans, religion was more significant than ethnicity or language. Since Balkan and Syrian Orthodox were subordinate to the Greek Orthodox patriarchs in Constantinople, Greeks had better prospects of advancement.[138] The Ottoman Empire's organization in itself was not ominous, but rather practical. When combined with other elements, however, these multi-polar un-mixing societies created a volatile environment that became evident during the decline of the empire.[139]

Symbolization

The Jesus Fish was used extensively in the Asia Minor region. ΙΧΘΥΣ literally means fish in Greek but it is also an acronym for Jesus Christ, God's Son our Savior (Ἰησοῦς Χριστός, Θεοῦ Υἱός, Σωτήρ). Churches in central Turkey are adorned with this symbol. Early Christians fearing persecution used it as a quasi-cryptic handshake when meeting others. One member would draw the top arch in the sand and the other (if Christian) would complete the fish by adding the bottom arch. Later of course, the symbol was replaced by the cross. Such self-imposed symbols have always been used in societies and are acceptable. Gregory Stanton specifically discusses symbols like customary dress that are explicitly imposed on a group to segregate them.

Various forms of imposed segregations existed in Ottoman Empire. The *dhimmi's* homes had to be painted a different color from Muslim homes. Edicts further dictated the specific color to be worn by each religious group. Jews wore turquoise, Greeks black

---

[138]Faroqhi, *Subjects of the Sultan*, 68.

[139]Akcam, *A Shameful Act*, 19-49.

76

while Armenians wore red shoes and headgear. It is unclear how or why the Ottomans selected the colors for the various groups. Interestingly the Orthodox priest (Papas) garb was also black, a self-imposed color. Limitations also extended to the clothes' materials. At times, non-Muslims were prohibited from wearing certain expensive or fine articles of clothing such as fur and silk. They were also forbidden from wearing clogs and had to wear small bells while in bathhouses. Once again, symbols in particularly dress were used to polarize the society into two groups and even dehumanize the minorities.[140]

Dehumanization

Stanton next states that classification and symbolization are fundamental measures in all cultures; however, they become steps to genocide only when combined with dehumanization. It is the denial of humanity that catalyzes the indiscriminate killing. According to Stanton, the natural abhorrence to murder is overcome by dehumanizing the victims. That said, victims are often mutilated, as in the case of Smyrna, to demonstrate the denial of humanity. Propaganda shows targeted groups as animals, weeds, diseases or other derogatory terms. In the Ottoman Empire names like "infidel pig" or "Gayour," a pejorative term for infidel, and other terms were used extensively for non-Muslims. Non-Muslim subjects of the Ottoman Empire were dehumanized in other ways as well.

In legal matters, non-Muslim testimonies against Muslims were not accepted in court. Non-Muslim men were also barred from marrying Muslim women. Christians and other minorities were not permitted to bear arms or ride horses. If travelling by foot they were required to step aside for approaching Muslims. Several restrictions also limited

---

[140]Ibid., 24-25.

77

home construction.[141] Non-Muslim homes could not be built near mosques and were in general discouraged from living within a town or near Muslim quarters.[142] They were also prohibited from building their houses higher than Muslim homes. In addition to painting their homes a different color, the windows of a Gayour's residence could not look over Muslim quarters.

Organization

Genocide always entails groups since it is based on group identity and segregation. The acts are traditionally organized by states, militias or hate groups. Such was the case in Turkey. Several sources indicate the central government's complicity in the outrages against both the Armenians and the Greeks of Pontus. Early on German Ambassador Baron von Wangenheim warned that if allied fleet forces the Dardanelles, the Turks would massacre their Christian populations.[143] This sentiment was echoed by Mehmed Talaat Pasha, Turkish Interior Minister. A Greek Patriarchate visited the Pasha to protest the atrocities committed by Talaat forces. Talaat responded by telling the cleric there was no room for Christians in Turkey and advised him to clear out the country and make room for Muslim refugees.[144] Once the massacres gained momentum, several sources witnessed governmental involvement.

---

[141]Ibid.

[142]Faroqhi, *Subjects of the Sultan*, 25.

[143]"Fear of General Massacre in Constantinople if Allied Fleet Passes Dardanelles," *The New York Times*, 9 January 1915.

[144]Ibid.

William Jennings Bryan, U.S. Secretary of State signed the following telegram

sent from the U.S. Embassy in Constantinople to the U.S. Department of State on May

29, 1915. The telegram reads as follows:

> French Foreign Office requests following notice be given Turkish Government.
> Quote. May 24th. For about a month the Kurd and Turkish population of Armenia
> has been massacring Armenians with the connivance and often assistance of
> Ottoman authorities. Such massacres took place in middle April (?) at Erzerum,
> Dertchun, Eguine, Akn, Bitlis, Mouch, Sassoun, Zeitoun, and through Cilicia.
> Inhabitants of about one hundred villages near Van were all murdered. In that city
> Armenian quarter is besieged by Kurds. At the same time in Constantinople
> government ill treats inoffensive Armenian population. In view of these new
> crimes of Turkey against humanity and civilization the Allied governments
> announce publicly to the Sublime Porte that they will hold personally responsible
> these crimes all members of the Ottoman government and those of their agents
> who are implicated in such massacres.[145]

The telegram clearly indicates Ottoman authorities assisting the massacres and

threatens punishment for their transgressions. Apparently, the threat was not enough to

dissuade them as four years later they organized pogroms once more, this time against the

Pontic Greeks. The Archibishop of Amassia and Samsoun sent a letter expressing his

concern for his people and was published in the *New York Times*. The prelate's letter also

indicates organized massacres in the one passage that reads:

> Euxine Pontus has undergone the greatest calamities and disaster, not only from
> the all-powerful Turkish Party of Union and Progress, but also from all the
> Turkish people. The Turkish people, after having hacked to death a million
> Armenians, organized and are still organizing according to the same methods,
> similar outrages. They were led, but only according to their own instincts, by the
> Government of Talaat, Enver, Djamal, and their accomplices.[146]

---

[145]The Armenian Genocide Museum-Institute, "France, Great Britain, and Russia Joint Declaration," 24 May 1915, http://www.genocide-museum.am/eng/France.php (accessed 8 May 2012).

[146]"Tells How Turks Tortured Greeks," *The New York Times*, 5 July 1919.

Polarization and Preparation

Polarization, according to Stanton, is the systemic elimination of moderates or anyone who may slow the killing cycle. At the same time, extremists work to drive the groups apart by implementing rules that prohibit intermarriage, as was the case here. Ottoman authorities targeted specific groups on the official day of Armenian Genocide, 24 April 1915. On this day, known as Red Sunday, the Ottoman government arrested and deported 250 Armenian intellectuals in Constantinople. The intellectuals were deported, most of which died from the process or were assassinated. Next Ottoman authorities did the same in other cities and towns rounding up Armenians, teachers, clergymen, and other leaders. Although Armenians had been persecuted centuries before, 24 April 1915 is designated the Genocide Remembrance Day, commemorating the notables' deportations. The event is seen as the commencement of the ensuing events. Later the Ottoman authorities used the exact same procedure with the Greeks of the Black Sea region.

Following polarization, preparation is the next step in genocide, which includes identification, expropriation of the victim's property, concentration of victims and finally transportation. The identification was easily addressed since the Ottomans had detailed lists of all the Rayas for taxation and other administrative reasons. Furthermore, as discussed in the symbolization paragraph, non-Muslims were relegated to specific dress and had certain housing requirements both of which made them easily identifiable. Unveiled Christian women were also clearly discernible from the others. So even if identification cards or lists were absent, the Christians could be easily and quickly identified by anyone familiar with local customs. Once the marauder identified their victims, they would gather them and expropriate the property and belongings before beginning transportation, usually by foot to the interior. As Archbishop Germanos wrote in a letter, "All the others after the pillage of their wealth, the confiscation of their homes and their cattle, were led away."[147]

A message dated 22 July 1916 from MB. N., identity unknown, communicated by the American committee for Armenian and Syrian Relief describes in vivid detail the deportation process. The American relief workers witnessed thousands of deported Armenians marching in "all phases of their miserable life." According to the report, the government issued insufficient rations. The victims thus resulted in eating grass, herbs, locust, dead animals and even human carcasses. Consequently, the maltreatment along with starvation and sickness resulted in extremely high death rates. The message ominously concludes, "the destruction from so-called natural causes seems decided upon."[148]

Extermination

Dr. Stanton uses the term extermination instead of murder or killings because in the eyes of the genocidaires the victims are not considered humans. Because of this distinction, it is acceptable to kill indiscriminately including women and children. As demonstrated by early examples, the extermination process of both Greeks and

---

[147]Ibid., Dan Bilefsky, "Turkey's Leader Counters French Law with Accusations of Colonial-Era Genocide," *The New York Times*, December 2011; Scott Sayare and Sebnem Arsu, "Genocide Bill Angers Turks as It Passes in France," *The New York Times*, 23 January 2012.

[148]ArmenianHouse.Org, "The Treatment of Armenians in the Ottoman Empire," http://armenianhouse.org/bryce/treatment/684-message.html (accessed 8 May 2012).

Armenians was extensively cruel, especially for peoples who had co-existed for centuries. The majority of the time the acts were executed by Ottomans who were outsiders, meaning individuals who did not know the victims. The local Muslims would often hide or otherwise protect their Christian neighbors, but those accounts are eclipsed by the atrocities. Few might have found the opportunity to get revenge for a previous grievance. Nevertheless, the soldiers' orders were to exterminate not just retaliate as evidence later proved.

During Solomon Teiliran's trial for Talaat Pasha's assassination, several pieces of evidence were introduced that clearly demonstrated the Turkish Army's intentions. An eyewitness gave testimony that Talaat Pasha's instructions ordering the deportations were "their destination is the void." Another witness testified he saw a telegram from Talaat to a high-ranking official that wanted to know how many were still alive. In addition, five messages with the Pasha's signature were introduced in evidence that stated, "remove the children from orphanages in order to eliminate future danger from antagonistic elements." The only thing more alarming and perplexing than the orders was that regular Turkish soldiers complied with Talaat. The soldiers, ordinary men, inhumanly tortured and watched the Armenians and Greeks perish on their march towards the void.[149]

The mechanics that compel ordinary people to commit such actions have been greatly debated mostly by scholars who studied the Jewish Holocaust. Three prominent genocide scholars, Goldhagen, Browning and Kuhne, suggest opposing explanations as to the way ordinary individuals can be spurred to commit genocide. Although all three scholars discuss only Germany and Nazi ideology, the conclusions they draw can be

---

[149]"Armenian Acquitted for Killing Talaat," *The New York Times*, 4 June 1921.

applied to all genocidaires. After all, it was the Armenian genocide that bolstered Hitler to go after the Jews. The German and Ottoman societies may differ greatly, but the insights of how to short-circuit individuals to commit genocide are the same regardless of the backdrop.

Professor Daniel Jonah Goldhagen, in *Hitler's Willing Executioners*, claims that anti-Semitism was pervasive in pre-Nazi Germany. When Hitler came to power, the Party's anti-Semitic sentiment mirrored the Germans' feelings and, therefore, Hitler simply unleashed the peoples' pre-existing hatred to perpetrate the Holocaust. Goldhagen claims the existence of anti-Semitism does not fluctuate in a society; it is omnipresent. The manifestations of such sentiments, however, change depending on circumstances. In that line of thinking, Goldhagen would claim Christian antipathy alone fueled the Ottoman atrocities. This position is myopic and hard to believe. A single factor alone cannot explain such a multifaceted and complex phenomenon.[150] Starkly opposed to this opinion, is Christopher R. Browning, author of *Ordinary Men*.

Professor Browning argues for a multilayered and a multi-causal explanation to mass atrocity motivators. According to the author, three groups emerged in Nazi Germany: eager killers, non-shooters (smallest group) and lastly, the largest group, comprised by those who did whatever they were asked to do in order to conform with authority and avoid appearing weak. This final group did not enjoy the brutality, but increasingly, had pity for themselves due to the unpleasant work they were forced to endure. As their actions were sanctioned by legitimate authority, they did not view their

---

[150]Daniel Jonah Goldhagen, *Hitler's Willing Executioners: Ordinary Germans and the Holocaust* (New York: Vintage, 1997).

83

activities as immoral or wrong. Finally, Browning claims the war itself served as a catalyst of the Holocaust as the Jews were seen as one of enemies that threatened the beleaguered Fatherland.[151] Browning's assertions are correct yet he fails to mention the group morality and shame culture prominent in Nazi Germany, which Professor Kuhne suggests, was an instrumental motivator.

Probably the most plausible explanation of "why" ordinary people committed atrocities is offered by Thomas Kuhne, author of *Perpetrators of the Holocaust*. Kuhne asserts that two forces working together, comradeship (sociology) and anti-Semitism (ideology), were the causative agents of the Holocaust. According to Kuhne, individual responsibility was displaced in Germany after World War I by a moral system that favored group good, also known as shame culture. Contrary to guilt cultures that emphasize individuals and individual responsibility, shame cultures are driven by comradeship and emphasize group or communal good. Comradeship exerts group pressure, brings social cohesion, and banishes individual thought. Ultimately, the group determines and defines moral or immoral actions, not individuals. With such pretexts, any actions authorized by the group are viewed as moral. Therefore, any sanctioned actions to protect the community from detrimental enemies, *vis-à-vis* Jews, Greeks or Armenians, are considered moral.[152]

---

[151]Christopher Browning, *Ordinary Men: Police Battalion 101 and the Final Solution in Poland* (New York: Harper Collins, 1998 reissued), 191-226.

[152]Thomas Kuhn, "Male Bonding and Shame Culture: Hitler's Soldiers and the Moral Basis of Genocidal Warfare," in *Ordinary People as Mass Murders*, edited by Olaf Jensen and Claus Christian W. Szejnmann (New York: Palgrave Macmillan), 55-74.

The extermination of Ottoman Christian population was possible because of the reasons both Kuhne and Browning support. As with the Holocaust, war was a catalyst for the atrocities. Unlike the Nazis however, the Ottomans were not the aggressors and they truly feared for their national existence. Though prejudices existed for non-Muslims, they were not the sole motive for the killings. Christians, Muslims and Jews all coexisted for several centuries under Ottoman rule with ambivalence. In fact Jews, enjoyed privilege unlike anywhere else. The relationship was so deep that many Jews claimed Mustafa Kemal Atatürk was actually Jewish.[153] He was after all born in Salonika, which thanks to the Ottomans was a primarily Jewish cosmopolitan city. It seems unreasonable then, that the Turks would embrace one religious minority yet persecute others. Therefore, it is doubtful that religious prejudice was the sole root of the animosity. Other aspects like the war played a much more significant role.

The backdrop of war exacerbated the exterminations. For one, the Turkish people worried for their nation's existence as they watched their homeland disintegrate and their armies defeated. Armenian communities suffered greatly for the defeat of Ottomans by the Russians. Since Ottoman Armenians occasionally supported the invading Russians, retaliation to an extent could be expected. Simultaneously, Turkish forces were aggressively engaged in a campaign in Gallipoli. The fears of the Ottomans were only worsened with the landing of Greek forces and the ensuing Greco-Turkish War. The main extermination culprits used the war to accomplish the murderous plans. Using the Black Sea coast's vulnerability to Russian attack as a pretext, the Turkish government started

---

[153]Hemingway, *Dateline: Toronto: Hemingway's Complete Toronto Star Dispatches 1920-1924*, 4184.

mass deportations of Pontic Greeks along with others, to the interior of the country. For these same reasons the Turkish government denies any allegations of genocide. Although the process of genocide is evident, the Turks claim the motives for the annihilation were for self-preservation and do not fit the genocide category.

Denial

Prometheus, according to mythology, pitied the cold humans so he stole fire from Zeus and gave it to mortals. In retaliation, Zeus bound Prometheus for eternity to a rock with an eagle gnawing at his liver, which continuously regenerated. The flame was used by humans for warmth, to cook meals, forge metals and aid overall progress towards civilization. In reality, the flame represents knowledge and has ever since been the symbol of enlightenment. Prometheus' punishment is also symbolic. While knowledge is empowering and liberating many fear it for those exact reasons. Such is the case with most perpetrators of genocide and mass atrocities. According to Dr. Stanton, every genocide is followed by denial. Most arguments against it use definitionalism, meaning they argue the definition of genocide.[154]

Turkey's stance on the Armenian Genocide is omnipresent even as recently as January 2012. Turkey ceased diplomatic and military relations with France after the Parliament backed a bill that would impose a fine and a year in jail for anyone who denies the Armenian Genocide. Turkey rebutted by asking France to look at its own

---

[154]Gregory H. Stanton, *The Eight Stages of Genocide*, First Working Paper (GS01) of the Yale Program in Genocide Studies, 1998.

history.[155] For Turkey, the events of 1915 were just a misfortunate consequence of a crumbling empire attacked by all sides and struggling to survive.[156] They reject the term genocide, arguing there was no premeditation and most of all no systematic attempt to destroy a people. Turkish historian Taner Akcam has written a book that, according to the publisher introduces "new evidence from more than 600 secret Ottoman documents, this book demonstrates in unprecedented detail the Armenian Genocide and the expulsion of Greeks from the late Ottoman Empire resulted from an official effort to rid the empire of its Christian subjects."[157] In the meantime, genocide scholars today are left with one lasting question. If the world had reacted differently to the Armenian Genocide, would Hitler have been reluctant to persecute the Jews?

---

[155]Bilefsky, "Turkey's Leader Counters French Law With Accusations of Colonial-Era Genocide."

[156]Sayare and Arsu, "Genocide Bill Angers Turks as It Passes in France."

[157]Taner Akcam, *The Young Turks' Crime Against Humanity,* http://www.amazon.com/Young-Turks-Crime-Against-Humanity/dp/0691153337/ ref=sr_1_1?s=books&ie=UTF8&qid=1334837458&sr=1-1 (accessed 19 April 2012).

CHAPTER 7

CONCLUSION

> To mention the name of Sherman to a Southerner of the United States is to fill him with burning indignation. Even the most ignorant yokel knows the name Attila is associated with untold horrors and vandalism. But the Smyrna affair, which far outweighs the horrors of the First World War or even the present one, has been somehow soft-pedaled and almost expunged from the memory of present-day man.
>
> — Henry Miller, *The Colossus of Maroussi*

In the Odyssey's preamble, Homer requests inspiration from a muse to commend the industrious Ulysses. Yet little inspiration is needed to praise Homer's hometown of Smyrna. This cosmopolitan city was once an epicenter of western civilization and later, Christianity. The city's prominence only continued under Ottoman rule becoming the empire's beacon of tolerance. In a tragic turn of events that beacon was extinguished by bloody conflict. The once vibrant city became as one reporter called it "a vast sepulcher of ashes."[158] The blame for the destruction of Smyrna is shouldered by many, not just the Turks who are accused of setting the city ablaze.

The primary blame for the destruction of Smyrna lies with the great powers, mainly Britain and France. These two powerful and duplicitous nations spurred the Greeks to start the Asia Minor Campaign, mostly for self-serving purposes. Once Mustafa Kemal resisted, the Allies either abandoned the Greeks or sided with the Turks. Guilt lies with the Greeks as their territorial aspirations initiated the Greco-Turkish war by occupying Smyrna. Finally, the Turks are to blame for the unrestrained killing spree

---

[158]"Smyrna's Ravagers Fired on Americans," *The New York Times*, 18 September 1922.

and ultimate burning of Smyrna. Most importantly the Smyrna holocaust and the events leading up to it, initiated the genocide machinations. The Greco-Turkish War and the Battle of Smyrna, exposed grievances and flared century-old animosities at great cost to human life and suffering. Thankfully, the population exchange and the ensuing peace treaty stopped the conflict and the potential genocide.

Today the exchange is both reviled and revered by scholars who have studied the subject. Critics claim it violated individuals' rights as politicians in the idyllic town of Lausanne sealed the destiny of 1.5 million people without their consent or input. In addition, the solution to the turmoil favored states instead of individual citizens. The Convention removed people from their ancestral homes ending centuries of cultural heritage. Most notably, those opposed to the convention argued that it set a dangerous precedent in which any nation with minority unrest would look for a similar solution of expulsion. Lastly, the population exchange had, as discussed, unprecedented and largely unexpected results on the societies and the nations involved. These critics, however, place more emphasis on the ethical considerations rather than the pragmatic results.[159]

The Treaty of Lausanne advocates laude it as one of the most durable of the twentieth century as it successfully ceased political and territorial disputes in the region.[160] The treaty ended the Greco-Turkish conflict and ensured a lasting peace in a relative volatile region. Although it violated individual rights, it ensured the survivability of those same individuals. As the delegates negotiating at Lausanne concluded, the population exchange was necessary to avoid future mass atrocities and potential

---

[159]Hirschon, *Crossing the Aegean*, 9-12.

[160]Ibid., 9.

genocide. The term genocide and its prerequisites were unknown to the statesmen at Lausanne, but their intuition indicated to the coming crime without a name.[161]

This paper set out to explore the thesis that the 1923 Greco-Turkish Population Exchange halted genocide of Greek Orthodox Christians living in Asia Minor. Firsthand historical records indicated the severity of the animosity between the Greek and Turkish populations prior to the Lausanne Convention. The Lausanne delegates' deliberations were greatly influenced by the Armenian Genocide and the Pontic Greek annihilation. Smyrna's holocaust was also still vivid in the delegates' memories. Based on the evidence available, the international community appropriately considered and implemented a population exchange in order to avert greater calamities despite the expected and unanticipated outcomes of that exchange. In most respects, there were no other viable options to preserve life and establish peace in the region—a peace that has held to this present day. The evidence provided in this paper supported the thesis.

Most important are the lessons garnered by the 1923 population exchange that can have universal implications. For one, the events leading to the exchange demonstrated that the international community cannot afford to vacillate when mass atrocities are committed. Inaction and indifference in the beginning result in substantial loss of blood and treasure for the nations involved and the international community. The League of Nations, the Refugee Settlement Commission, the Near East Relief and the countless other international relief originations were not funded by either Greece or Turkey, but by benevolent nations and citizens. The population exchange also demonstrated that world leaders have yet another choice when evaluating options for nations that have minority

---

[161]Bent, "Uprooting of Greeks in Turkey A Modern Exodus of Outcasts."

problems, especially in conflicts in those nations that can lead to mass atrocities and possibly genocide. When evaluating potential solutions to genocide prevention all possibilities must be exhausted especially in the operational environments of today and the future.

According to the U.S. Army's Field Manual 3-0, *Operations*, the future will be filled with persistent conflict due to urbanization, overpopulation, failing nation states, scarcity of resources, globalization, climate change and natural disasters, technology, and proliferation of weapons of mass destruction.[162] In the complex future plagued by overpopulation and resource restrictions, forced population migration, although not ideal, may be the only crisis solution. Although deracinating people from their ancestral homes is not preferred, it is pragmatic and effective. Most of the time conflict in the region already forces populations to flee for safety, so a population exchange or move may not be as draconian as it seems. This certainly was the case with the Greco-Turkish war.

The Balkan Wars of 1912 and 1913 and then World War I resulted in millions of displaced personnel before the population exchange was completed. It is estimated that the last months of 1922 before the Lausanne Convention was agreed, over one million refugees had arrived in Greece from Asia Minor and the surrounding region.[163] The Lausanne Convention simply provided the legal framework for the climax of an ongoing process.[164] Even in other conflicts following the Greco-Turkish exchange, nations were

---

[162]US Department of the Army, FM 3-0, *Operations* (Washington, DC: Government Printing Office, February 2008), 1-1-1-3.

[163]Ibid., 6.

[164]Ibid., 4.

91

deracinating people often using the Lausanne Convention as an example. The Nazi negotiated several population exchanges with the Italians and Soviet Russia during their short-lived alliance 1939 to 1941. After the Second World War, up to 12 million Germans were deported from Eastern Europe to Allied-Occupied Germany. Winston Churchill and Franklin Roosevelt modeled those actions from the removal of Orthodox Christians from Anatolia.[165] Such population "unmixing," in Lord Curzon's words, certainly has negative consequences.[166]

The individuals affected by the Lausanne Convention have poignant stories to tell. It is undoubtedly a tragedy to uproot a culture that flourished and existed in coastal Turkey since the time of Homer. It is also understandable then that those exchanged would forever long for their Ithaca. The Greek playwright Euripides lamented "there is no greater sorrow on earth than the loss of one's native land." The children of the Lausanne treaty would probably disagree arguing that it is better to relinquish your ancestral lands than be buried on them. The greatness of a culture is not found in columns, artifacts or other tangible goods. The true treasure of any nation is the citizens imbued with the culture, customs and ancestral heritage. Aristotle Onassis, Gabriel Isaakides and over a million other individuals survived because of the exchange. Without them, their story would have never been told, a fate far worse than hollow buildings on a mountainside.

---

[165]Clark, *Twice a Stranger*, xiii.

[166]Hirschon, *Crossing the Aegean*, 4.

APPENDIX A

Geography Terms

Anatolia: Term used in contemporary Turkish to describe the same land mass as Asia Minor. Anatolia is actually a Greek word but it is almost never used by Greeks.[167]

Asia Minor: Term used mostly by Greeks (*Mikra Asia, Mikrasia*) and refers to the land mass which comprises the major part of Asiatic Turkey today.[168]

Crete: Is Greece's largest island, located just south of the mainland. Crete was home to the Minoans, the earliest ancient Greek civilization. Cretans are bellicose and proud of their heritage-comparable to Texans. While mainland Greece was under Ottoman rule for 400 years, Crete's occupation lasted 200 years. Crete is also the birthplace of Eleftherios Venizelos. NOTE: Crete is not Cyprus.[169]

Ionia: An ancient Greek region of central coastal Asia Minor/Anatolia in present-day Turkey. The Ionian region encompasses the city of Smyrna (Izmir). Ionia was a culturally and resource wealthy region. Thales from the Ionian School of philosophy is considered the earliest western philosopher. He originated the scientific thought by finding naturalistic explanations to phenomena without supernatural references. Furthermore, the Ionic order of architecture and Homer are also Ionian. Because of its history, the region is interwoven with the Greek psyche and thus greatly coveted. In fact, the Arabic, Turkish, Persian and Urdu name for Greece is Younan, a transliteration of Ionia.

Kavala: Is a city in northern Greece near Salonika/Thessaloniki. Kavala is in the region of Greek Macedonia.

Macedonia: Is the region centered in the northeastern part of the Greek peninsula. In antiquity, the Macedonian Kingdom encompassed territory found in many modern nations (including Former Yugoslav Republic of Macedonia). By all accounts, the Macedonians were Hellenes meaning Greeks. Today the majority of the territory and the capital of ancient Macedonia (Pella) are found in modern Greece. For these reasons, Greece strongly contested the naming of the modern nation of Macedonia. Modern Greece still calls its northeastern provenance Macedonia. Thessaloniki/Salonika, Kavala and Fort Rupel are all in the Greek region of Macedonia.

---

[167]Hirschon, *Crossing the Aegean*, xi-xiii.

[168]Ibid.

[169]Greeka.com, "The Greek Island Specialist," http://www.greeka.com/ crete/index.htm (accessed 6 May 2012).

Smyrna (Izmir): Is the ancient Greek city in Ionia. Contemporary Greeks still call the city Smyrna. In Turkish, the city is called Izmir. Historically, the Turks referred to the city as gavur Izmir (infidel Izmir) because of its large non-Muslim population. Smyrna/Izmir was the culminating point of the Greco-Turkish War (1919-1922).[170]

Thessaloniki (Salonika): Is Greece's second largest city located in the northern region of Macedonia. The words Thessaloniki and Salonika are used interchangeably. Allied forces withdrawing from the Gallipoli Campaign amassed in the city of Salonika without Greek approval. Exploiting Greece's lack of means to resist and attempts to remain neutral, Greek sovereignty was often violated by both sides during World War I. Salonika is also the birthplace of Mustafa Kemal Atatürk, which at the time of his birth was under Ottoman rule.

---

[170]Milton, *Paradise Lost*, 331-333.

APPENDIX B

Consent and Use Agreement for Oral History Material

CONSENT AND USE AGREEMENT FOR ORAL HISTORY MATERIALS

You have the right to choose whether or not you will participate in this oral history interview, and once you begin you may cease participating at any time without penalty. The anticipated risk to you in participating is negligible and no direct personal benefit has been offered for your participation. If you have questions about this research study, please contact the student at:_____
or Dr. Robert F. Baumann, Director of Graduate Degree Programs, at (913) 684-2742.

To: Director, Graduate Degree Programs
Room 4508, Lewis & Clark Center
U.S. Army Command and General Staff College

1. I, ANASTASIA ISAAKIDOU , participated in an oral history interview conducted by

JASON B. FAULKENBERRY, a graduate student in the Master of Military Art and Science

Degree Program, on the following date [s]: 30 April 2012 concerning the

following topic: FATHER GABRIEL DURING 1923 Population Exchange.

2. I understand that the recording [s] and any transcript resulting from this oral history will belong to the U.S. Government to be used in any manner deemed in the best interests of the Command and General Staff College or the U.S. Army, in accordance with guidelines posted by the Director, Graduate Degree Programs and the Center for Military History. I also understand that subject to security classification restrictions I will be provided with a copy of the recording for my professional records. In addition, prior to the publication of any complete edited transcript of this oral history, I will be afforded an opportunity to verify its accuracy.

3. I hereby expressly and voluntarily relinquish all rights and interests in the recording [s] with the following caveat:

____✓____ None _____ Other: _____

I understand that my participation in this oral history interview is voluntary and I may stop participating at any time without explanation or penalty. I understand that the tapes and transcripts resulting from this oral history may be subject to the Freedom of Information Act, and therefore, may be releasable to the public contrary to my wishes. I further understand that, within the limits of the law, the U.S. Army will attempt to honor the restrictions I have requested to be placed on these materials.

ANASTASIA ISAAKIDOU   Anastasia Isaakidou   30 APRIL 2012
Name of Interviewee   Signature   Date

FAULKENBERRY, JASON MAJ, MS   30 APRIL 2012
Accepted on Behalf of the Army by   Date

BIBLIOGRAPHY

Books

Afetinan, A. *A History of the Turkish Revolution and Turkish Republic*. Ankara, Turkey, 1981.

Akcam, Taner. *A Shameful Act: The Armenian Genocide and the Question of Turkish Responsibility*. New York: Holt Paperbacks, 2006.

Alexander, Edward. *A Crime of Vengeance: An Armenian Struggel for Justice*. New York: The Free Prees, 1991.

Alexandris, Alexis. "Religion or Ethinicity: Identity of the Minorities." In *Crossing the Aegean: An Appraisal of the 1923 Compulsory Population Exchange Between Greece and Turkey*, edited by Renee Hirschon, 116-132. New York: Oxford, 2008.

Bideleux, Robert, and Ian Jeffries. *A History of Eastern Europe: Crisis and Change*. New York: Routledge, 2007.

Clark, Bruce. *Twice a Stranger: The mass expulsions that Forged Modern Greece and Turkey*. Cambridge: Harvard University Press, 2006.

Clogg, Richard. *A Concise History of Greece*. Cambridge: Cambridge University Press, 1992.

Colonas, Vassilis. "Housing and the Architectural Expression of Asia Minor Greeks Before and After 1923." In *Crossing the Aegean An Appraisal of the 1923 Compusory Population Exchange Between Greece and Turkey*, edited by Renee Hirschon, 163-178. New York: Oxford, 2008.

Curtis, Glenn E., ed., Federal Research Division Library of Congress, producer. *Greece: A Country Study*. 4th ed. Washington, DC: Department of the Army, 1995.

Dalby, Andrew. *Eleftherios Venizelos: Greece*. London: Haus Publishing, 2010.

Dobkin, Marjorie Housepian. *Smyrna 1922: The Destruction of a City*. New York: Newmark Press, 1998.

Faroqhi, Suraiya. *Subjects of the Sultan*. New York: I. B.Tauris and Co. Ltd., 2007.

Goldhagen, Daniel Jonah. *Hitler's Willing Executioners: Ordinary Germans and the Holocaust*. New York: Vintage, 1997.

Halo, Thea. *Not Even my Name*. New York: Picardo, 2001.

Hemingway, Ernest. *Dateline: Toronto: Hemingway's Complete Toronto Star Dispatches 1920-1924.* New York: Charles Scribner's Sons, 1985.

————. *In Our Time.* New York: Scribner, 2002.

Hirschon, Renee. *Crossing the Aegean: An Appraisal of the 1923 Compulsory Population Exchange Between Greece and Turkey.* New York: Oxford, 2008.

Horton, George. *The Blight of Asia: An account of the systematic extermination of Christian populations by Mohammedans and of the culpability of certain great powers; With a true story of the burning of Smyrna.* Indianapolis: Bobbs-Merrill, 1926.

Howard, Harry N. *The Partition of Turkey: A Diplomatic History, 1913-1923.* Norman, OK: University of Oklahoma Press, 1931.

Kasaba, Resat. "Izmir 1922: A Port City Unravels." In *Modernity and Culture*, edited by Leila Tarazi Fawa and C. A. Bayly, 204-229. New York: Columbia University Press, 2002.

Kuhn, Thomas. "Male Bonding and Shame Culture: Hitler's Soldiers and the Moral Basis of Genocidal Warfare." In *Ordinary People as Mass Murders*, edited by Olaf Jensen and Claus Christian W. Szejnmann 55-74. New York: Palgrave Macmillan.

Lansing, Robert. *The Big Four and Others of the Peace Conference.* 1921. Reprint, Cornell University Library, 2009.

Levitsky, Ronald. *The Pontian Greek Genocide: A Teaching Unit.* Chicago: Pontian Society of Chicago, 2006.

Lewis, Geoffrey L. *Modern Turkey.* New York: Praeger, 1974.

Luke, Sir Harry. *The Old Turkey and the New: From Byzantium to Ankara.* London: Bles, 1955.

Milton, Giles. *Paradise Lost: Smyrna 1922: The Destruction of a Christian City in the Islamic World.* New York: Basic Books, 2008.

Nicolle, David. *Armies of the Ottoman Turks 1300-1774.* London: Osprey, 1983.

Power, Samantha. *A Problem from Hell: America and the Age of Genocide.* New York: Harper Perennial, 2003.

Smothers, Frank, William Hardy McNeill, and Elizabeth Darbishire McNeill. *Report on the Greeks: Findings of a Twentieth Century Fund team which surveyed conditions in Greece in 1947.* New York: The Twentieth Century Fund, 1948.

Stanton, Gregory H. *The Eight Stages of Genocide.* Washington, DC: Genocide Watch, 1998.

Torumtay, Necip. *Atatürk.* Ankara: Turkiye Cumhuriyeti Genelkurmay Ba'skanli gi Basimevi, 1981.

Vook, Dr. *The Byzantine Empire 101: The Textvook.* Vook, 2011.

Periodicals

"Allies in Agreement on Lausanne Demands." *The New York Times,* 17 November 1922.

"Armenian Acquitted for Killing Talaat." *The New York Times*, 4 June 1921.

"Convention concerning the exchange of Greek and Turkish populations." *The American Journal of International Law* 18, no. 2 (1924): 84-90.

"Fear of General Massacre in Constantinople if Allied Fleet Passes Dardanelles." *The New York Times*, 9 January 1915.

"Smyrna's Ravagers Fired on Americans." *The New York Times,* 18 September 1922.

"Talaat Pasha Slain in Berlin Suburb." *The New York Times*, 16 March 1921.

"Tells How Turks Tortured Greeks." *The New York Times*, 5 July 1919.

"Woman Pictures Smyrna Horrors." *The New York Times*, 8 October 1922.

"Venizelos Shot, Twice Wounded by Greeks in Paris." *The New York Times*, 13 August 1920.

Bent, Silas. "Uprooting of Greeks in Turkey A Modern Exodus of Outcasts." *The New York Times*, 21 January 1923.

Bilefsky, Dan. "Turkey's Leader Counters French Law With Accusations of Colonial-Era Genocide." *The New York Times*, December 2011.

James, Edwin L. "American Envoy Asks Guarantees for Minorities." *The New York Times*, 13 December 1922.

———. "Kemal Won't Insure Against Massacres." *The New York Times*, 11 September 1922.

———. "Million Must Quit Homes in Near East Lausanne Decrees." *The New York Times*, 11 January 1923.

————. "Turks Proclaim Banishment Edict to 1,000,000 Greeks." *The New York Times*, 2 December 1922.

Mazower, M. "The messiah and the bourgeoisie: Venizelos and politics in Greece, 1909-1912." *The Historical Journal* 35, no. 4 (1992): 885-904.

Sayare, Scott, and Sebnem Arsu. "Genocide Bill Angers Turks as It Passes in France." *The New York Times*, 23 January 2012.

Internet Sources

Armenian Genocide. "Recognition." http://www.mtholyoke.edu/~kotik22a/classweb/armenian_genocide/why_matters.html (accessed 18 April 2012).

Armenian Genocide Museum-Institute. "France, Great Britain, and Russia Joint Declaration," 24 May 1915. http://www.genocide-museum.am/eng/France.php (accessed 8 May 2012).

Greek-Genocide.org. "Greek Genocide 1914-23." http://www.greek-genocide.org pontus.html (accessed 18 April 2012).

Hulse, Caroline. "Ernest Hemingway." http://www.ernest.hemingway.com/Elizabethhadley.htm (accessed 5 April 2012).

Lexicon of Greek Personal Names. "The Transition to Modern Greek Names." http://www.lgpn.ox.ac.uk/names/modern.html (accessed 30 April 2012).

Patterson, Michael R. "Arlington National Cemetery." 25 September 2000. http://www.arlingtoncemetery.net/gdilboy.htm (accessed 5 April 2012).

Schulweis, Harold M. "Human Rights in Crises: A Summary for Jewish World Watch." JewishWorldWatch.org. 2 June 2008. http://www.jewishworldwatch.org/wp-content/uploads/2010/06/wc_Jun2008.pdf (accessed 18 April 2012).

Stanton, Gregory H. "What is Genocide?" *Genocide Watch.* http://www.genocide watch.org/genocide/whatisit.html (accessed 18 April 2012).

Ward, Mark H., and Forrest D. Yowell. "Archival Document Project." *Greek-Genocide.org.* 5 April 1922. http://www.greek-genocide.org/documents.html (accessed 18 April 2012).

Other Sources

Isaakidou, Anastasia, daughter of Gabriel Isaakidou. Interview by Jason Faulkenberry, 30 April 2012.

Lausanne Peace Treaty VI. Convention concerning the Exchange of Greek and Turkish Populations and Protocol, signed at Lausanne 30 January 1923.

US Department of the Army. FM 3-0, *Operations.* Washington, DC: Government Printing Office, February 2008.